Nutshell Series
Hornbook Series

and

Black Letter Series

of

WEST PUBLISHING COMPANY
P.O. Box 64526
St. Paul, Minnesota 55164–0526

Accounting

FARIS' ACCOUNTING AND LAW IN A NUTSHELL, 377 pages, 1984. Softcover. (Text)

Administrative Law

GELLHORN AND LEVIN'S ADMINISTRATIVE LAW AND PROCESS IN A NUTSHELL, Third Edition, approximately 420 pages, 1990. Softcover. (Text)

Admiralty

MARAIST'S ADMIRALTY IN A NUTSHELL, Second Edition, 379 pages, 1988. Softcover. (Text)

SCHOENBAUM'S HORNBOOK ON ADMIRALTY AND MARITIME LAW, Student Edition, 692 pages, 1987 with 1989 pocket part. (Text)

Agency—Partnership

REUSCHLEIN AND GREGORY'S HORNBOOK ON THE LAW OF AGENCY AND PARTNERSHIP, Second Edition, 683 pages, 1990. (Text)

STEFFEN'S AGENCY-PARTNERSHIP IN A NUTSHELL, 364 pages, 1977. Softcover. (Text)

American Indian Law

CANBY'S AMERICAN INDIAN LAW IN A NUTSHELL, Second Edition, 336 pages, 1988. Softcover. (Text)

Antitrust—see also Regulated Industries, Trade Regulation

GELLHORN'S ANTITRUST LAW AND ECONOMICS IN A NUTSHELL, Third Edition, 472

List current as of July, 1990

Antitrust—Continued

pages, 1986. Softcover. (Text)

HOVENKAMP'S BLACK LETTER ON ANTITRUST, 323 pages, 1986. Softcover. (Review)

HOVENKAMP'S HORNBOOK ON ECONOMICS AND FEDERAL ANTITRUST LAW, Student Edition, 414 pages, 1985. (Text)

SULLIVAN'S HORNBOOK OF THE LAW OF ANTITRUST, 886 pages, 1977. (Text)

Appellate Advocacy—see Trial and Appellate Advocacy

Art Law

DUBOFF'S ART LAW IN A NUTSHELL, 335 pages, 1984. Softcover. (Text)

Banking Law

LOVETT'S BANKING AND FINANCIAL INSTITUTIONS LAW IN A NUTSHELL, Second Edition, 464 pages, 1988. Softcover. (Text)

Civil Procedure—see also Federal Jurisdiction and Procedure

CLERMONT'S BLACK LETTER ON CIVIL PROCEDURE, Second Edition, 332 pages, 1988. Softcover. (Review)

FRIEDENTHAL, KANE AND MILLER'S HORNBOOK ON CIVIL PROCEDURE, 876 pages, 1985. (Text)

KANE'S CIVIL PROCEDURE IN A NUTSHELL, Second Edition, 306 pages, 1986. Softcover. (Text)

KOFFLER AND REPPY'S HORNBOOK ON COMMON LAW PLEADING, 663 pages, 1969. (Text)

SIEGEL'S HORNBOOK ON NEW YORK PRACTICE, 1011 pages, 1978, with 1987 pocket part. (Text)

Commercial Law

BAILEY AND HAGEDORN'S SECURED TRANSACTIONS IN A NUTSHELL, Third Edition, 390 pages, 1988. Softcover. (Text)

HENSON'S HORNBOOK ON SECURED TRANSACTIONS UNDER THE U.C.C., Second Edition, 504 pages, 1979, with 1979 pocket part. (Text)

NICKLES' BLACK LETTER ON COMMERCIAL PAPER, 450 pages, 1988. Softcover. (Review)

SPEIDEL'S BLACK LETTER ON SALES AND SALES FINANCING, 363 pages, 1984. Softcover. (Review)

STOCKTON'S SALES IN A NUT-

Commercial Law—Continued

SHELL, Second Edition, 370 pages, 1981. Softcover. (Text)

STONE'S UNIFORM COMMERCIAL CODE IN A NUTSHELL, Third Edition, 580 pages, 1989. Softcover. (Text)

WEBER AND SPEIDEL'S COMMERCIAL PAPER IN A NUTSHELL, Third Edition, 404 pages, 1982. Softcover. (Text)

WHITE AND SUMMERS' HORNBOOK ON THE UNIFORM COMMERCIAL CODE, Third Edition, Student Edition, 1386 pages, 1988. (Text)

Community Property

MENNELL AND BOYKOFF'S COMMUNITY PROPERTY IN A NUTSHELL, Second Edition, 432 pages, 1988. Softcover. (Text)

Comparative Law

GLENDON, GORDON AND OSAKWE'S COMPARATIVE LEGAL TRADITIONS IN A NUTSHELL. 402 pages, 1982. Softcover. (Text)

Conflict of Laws

HAY'S BLACK LETTER ON CONFLICT OF LAWS, 330 pages, 1989. Softcover. (Review)

SCOLES AND HAY'S HORNBOOK ON CONFLICT OF LAWS, Student Edition, 1085 pages, 1982, with 1988–89 pocket part. (Text)

SEIGEL'S CONFLICTS IN A NUTSHELL, 470 pages, 1982. Softcover. (Text)

Constitutional Law—Civil Rights

BARRON AND DIENES' BLACK LETTER ON CONSTITUTIONAL LAW, Second Edition, 310 pages, 1987. Softcover. (Review)

BARRON AND DIENES' CONSTITUTIONAL LAW IN A NUTSHELL, 389 pages, 1986. Softcover. (Text)

ENGDAHL'S CONSTITUTIONAL FEDERALISM IN A NUTSHELL, Second Edition, 411 pages, 1987. Softcover. (Text)

MARKS AND COOPER'S STATE CONSTITUTIONAL LAW IN A NUTSHELL, 329 pages, 1988. Softcover. (Text)

NOWAK, ROTUNDA AND YOUNG'S HORNBOOK ON CONSTITUTIONAL LAW, Third Edition, 1191 pages, 1986 with 1988 pocket part. (Text)

VIEIRA'S CONSTITUTIONAL CIVIL RIGHTS IN A NUTSHELL, Second Edition, 322 pages, 1990. Softcover. (Text)

Constitutional Law—Civil Rights—Continued

WILLIAMS' CONSTITUTIONAL ANALYSIS IN A NUTSHELL, 388 pages, 1979. Softcover. (Text)

Consumer Law—see also Commercial Law

EPSTEIN AND NICKLES' CONSUMER LAW IN A NUTSHELL, Second Edition, 418 pages, 1981. Softcover. (Text)

Contracts

CALAMARI AND PERILLO'S BLACK LETTER ON CONTRACTS, Second Edition, approximately 450 pages, 1990. Softcover. (Review)

CALAMARI AND PERILLO'S HORNBOOK ON CONTRACTS, Third Edition, 1049 pages, 1987. (Text)

CORBIN'S TEXT ON CONTRACTS, One Volume Student Edition, 1224 pages, 1952. (Text)

FRIEDMAN'S CONTRACT REMEDIES IN A NUTSHELL, 323 pages, 1981. Softcover. (Text)

KEYES' GOVERNMENT CONTRACTS IN A NUTSHELL, Second Edition, approximately 530 pages, 1990. Softcover. (Text)

SCHABER AND ROHWER'S CON-

TRACTS IN A NUTSHELL, Third Edition, approximately 438 pages, 1990. Softcover. (Text)

Copyright—see Patent and Copyright Law

Corporations

HAMILTON'S BLACK LETTER ON CORPORATIONS, Second Edition, 513 pages, 1986. Softcover. (Review)

HAMILTON'S THE LAW OF CORPORATIONS IN A NUTSHELL, Second Edition, 515 pages, 1987. Softcover. (Text)

HENN AND ALEXANDER'S HORNBOOK ON LAWS OF CORPORATIONS, Third Edition, Student Edition, 1371 pages, 1983, with 1986 pocket part. (Text)

Corrections

KRANTZ' THE LAW OF CORRECTIONS AND PRISONERS' RIGHTS IN A NUTSHELL, Third Edition, 407 pages, 1988. Softcover. (Text)

Creditors' Rights

EPSTEIN'S DEBTOR-CREDITOR RELATIONS IN A NUTSHELL, Third Edition, 383 pages, 1986. Softcover. (Text)

NICKLES AND EPSTEIN'S BLACK LETTER ON CREDITORS' RIGHTS AND BANKRUPTCY, 576 pages,

Environmental Law—Continued

pages, 1988. Softcover. (Text)

RODGERS' HORNBOOK ON ENVIRONMENTAL LAW, 956 pages, 1977, with 1984 pocket part. (Text)

Equity—see Remedies

Estate Planning—see also Trusts and Estates; Taxation—Estate and Gift

LYNN'S AN INTRODUCTION TO ESTATE PLANNING IN A NUTSHELL, Third Edition, 370 pages, 1983. Softcover. (Text)

Evidence

BROUN AND BLAKEY'S BLACK LETTER ON EVIDENCE, 269 pages, 1984. Softcover. (Review)

GRAHAM'S FEDERAL RULES OF EVIDENCE IN A NUTSHELL, Second Edition, 473 pages, 1987. Softcover. (Text)

LILLY'S AN INTRODUCTION TO THE LAW OF EVIDENCE, Second Edition, 585 pages, 1987. (Text)

MCCORMICK'S HORNBOOK ON EVIDENCE, Third Edition, Student Edition, 1156 pages, 1984, with 1987 pocket part. (Text)

ROTHSTEIN'S EVIDENCE IN A NUTSHELL: STATE AND FEDERAL RULES, Second Edition, 514 pages, 1981. Softcover. (Text)

Federal Jurisdiction and Procedure

CURRIE'S FEDERAL JURISDICTION IN A NUTSHELL, Third Edition, approximately 260 pages, 1990. Softcover. (Text)

REDISH'S BLACK LETTER ON FEDERAL JURISDICTION, 219 pages, 1985. Softcover. (Review)

WRIGHT'S HORNBOOK ON FEDERAL COURTS, Fourth Edition, Student Edition, 870 pages, 1983. (Text)

Future Interests—see Trusts and Estates

Health Law—see Medicine, Law and

Human Rights—see International Law

Immigration Law

WEISSBRODT'S IMMIGRATION LAW AND PROCEDURE IN A NUTSHELL, Second Edition, 438 pages, 1989, Softcover. (Text)

Indian Law—see American Indian Law

Insurance Law

DOBBYN'S INSURANCE LAW IN A NUTSHELL, Second Edition, 316 pages, 1989. Softcover. (Text)

KEETON AND WIDISS' INSURANCE LAW, Student Edition, 1359 pages, 1988. (Text)

International Law—see also Sea, Law of

BUERGENTHAL'S INTERNATIONAL HUMAN RIGHTS IN A NUTSHELL, 283 pages, 1988. Softcover. (Text)

BUERGENTHAL AND MAIER'S PUBLIC INTERNATIONAL LAW IN A NUTSHELL, Second Edition, 275 pages, 1990. Softcover. (Text)

FOLSOM, GORDON AND SPANOGLE'S INTERNATIONAL BUSINESS TRANSACTIONS IN A NUTSHELL, Third Edition, 509 pages, 1988. Softcover. (Text)

Interviewing and Counseling

SHAFFER AND ELKINS' LEGAL INTERVIEWING AND COUNSELING IN A NUTSHELL, Second Edition, 487 pages, 1987. Softcover. (Text)

Introduction to Law—see Legal Method and Legal System

Introduction to Law Study

HEGLAND'S INTRODUCTION TO THE STUDY AND PRACTICE OF LAW IN A NUTSHELL, 418 pages, 1983. Softcover. (Text)

KINYON'S INTRODUCTION TO LAW STUDY AND LAW EXAMINATIONS IN A NUTSHELL, 389 pages, 1971. Softcover. (Text)

Judicial Process—see Legal Method and Legal System

Juvenile Justice

FOX'S JUVENILE COURTS IN A NUTSHELL, Third Edition, 291 pages, 1984. Softcover. (Text)

Labor and Employment Law—see also Employment Discrimination, Social Legislation

LESLIE'S LABOR LAW IN A NUTSHELL, Second Edition, 397 pages, 1986. Softcover. (Text)

NOLAN'S LABOR ARBITRATION LAW AND PRACTICE IN A NUTSHELL, 358 pages, 1979. Softcover. (Text)

Land Finance—Property Security—see Real Estate Transactions

Land Use

HAGMAN AND JUERGENS-MEYER'S HORNBOOK ON URBAN PLANNING AND LAND DEVELOPMENT CONTROL LAW, Second Edition, Student Edition, 680 pages, 1986. (Text)

WRIGHT AND WRIGHT'S LAND USE IN A NUTSHELL, Second Edition, 356 pages, 1985. Softcover. (Text)

Legal Method and Legal System—see also Legal Research, Legal Writing

KEMPIN'S HISTORICAL INTRODUCTION TO ANGLO-AMERICAN LAW IN A NUTSHELL, Third Edition, approximately 302 pages, 1990. Softcover. (Text)

REYNOLDS' JUDICIAL PROCESS IN A NUTSHELL, 292 pages, 1980. Softcover. (Text)

Legal Research

COHEN'S LEGAL RESEARCH IN A NUTSHELL, Fourth Edition, 452 pages, 1985. Softcover. (Text)

COHEN, BERRING AND OLSON'S HOW TO FIND THE LAW, Ninth Edition, 716 pages, 1989. (Text)

Legal Writing

SQUIRES AND ROMBAUER'S LEGAL WRITING IN A NUTSHELL, 294 pages, 1982. Softcover. (Text)

Legislation

DAVIES' LEGISLATIVE LAW AND PROCESS IN A NUTSHELL, Second Edition, 346 pages, 1986. Softcover. (Text)

Local Government

MCCARTHY'S LOCAL GOVERNMENT LAW IN A NUTSHELL, Third Edition, approximately 400 pages, 1990. Softcover. (Text)

REYNOLDS' HORNBOOK ON LOCAL GOVERNMENT LAW, 860 pages, 1982, with 1990 pocket part. (Text)

Mass Communication Law

ZUCKMAN, GAYNES, CARTER AND DEE'S MASS COMMUNICATIONS LAW IN A NUTSHELL, Third Edition, 538 pages, 1988. Softcover. (Text)

Medicine, Law and

HALL AND ELLMAN'S HEALTH CARE LAW AND ETHICS IN A NUTSHELL, 401 pages, 1990. Softcover (Text)

KING'S THE LAW OF MEDICAL MALPRACTICE IN A NUTSHELL,

Medicine, Law and—Continued

Second Edition, 342 pages, 1986. Softcover. (Text)

Military Law

SHANOR AND TERRELL'S MILITARY LAW IN A NUTSHELL, 378 pages, 1980. Softcover. (Text)

Mortgages—see Real Estate Transactions

Natural Resources Law—see Energy and Natural Resources Law, Environmental Law

Office Practice—see also Computers and Law, Interviewing and Counseling, Negotiation

HEGLAND'S TRIAL AND PRACTICE SKILLS IN A NUTSHELL, 346 pages, 1978. Softcover (Text)

Oil and Gas—see also Energy and Natural Resources Law

HEMINGWAY'S HORNBOOK ON OIL AND GAS, Second Edition, Student Edition, 543 pages, 1983, with 1989 pocket part. (Text)

LOWE'S OIL AND GAS LAW IN A NUTSHELL, Second Edition, 465 pages, 1988. Softcover. (Text)

Partnership—see Agency—Partnership

Patent and Copyright Law

MILLER AND DAVIS' INTELLECTUAL PROPERTY—PATENTS, TRADEMARKS AND COPYRIGHT IN A NUTSHELL, Second Edition, approximately 440 pages, 1990. Softcover. (Text)

Products Liability

PHILLIPS' PRODUCTS LIABILITY IN A NUTSHELL, Third Edition, 307 pages, 1988. Softcover. (Text)

Professional Responsibility

ARONSON AND WECKSTEIN'S PROFESSIONAL RESPONSIBILITY IN A NUTSHELL, 399 pages, 1980. Softcover. (Text)

ROTUNDA'S BLACK LETTER ON PROFESSIONAL RESPONSIBILITY, Second Edition, 414 pages, 1988. Softcover. (Review)

WOLFRAM'S HORNBOOK ON MODERN LEGAL ETHICS, Student Edition, 1120 pages, 1986. (Text)

Property—see also Real Estate Transactions, Land Use, Trusts and Estates

BERNHARDT'S BLACK LETTER ON PROPERTY, 318 pages, 1983. Softcover. (Review)

Property—Continued

BERNHARDT'S REAL PROPERTY IN A NUTSHELL, Second Edition, 448 pages, 1981. Softcover. (Text)

BURKE'S PERSONAL PROPERTY IN A NUTSHELL, 322 pages, 1983. Softcover. (Text)

CUNNINGHAM, STOEBUCK AND WHITMAN'S HORNBOOK ON THE LAW OF PROPERTY, Student Edition, 916 pages, 1984, with 1987 pocket part. (Text)

HILL'S LANDLORD AND TENANT LAW IN A NUTSHELL, Second Edition, 311 pages, 1986. Softcover. (Text)

Real Estate Transactions

BRUCE'S REAL ESTATE FINANCE IN A NUTSHELL, Second Edition, 262 pages, 1985. Softcover. (Text)

NELSON AND WHITMAN'S BLACK LETTER ON LAND TRANSACTIONS AND FINANCE, Second Edition, 466 pages, 1988. Softcover. (Review)

NELSON AND WHITMAN'S HORN-BOOK ON REAL ESTATE FINANCE LAW, Second Edition, 941 pages, 1985 with 1989 pocket part. (Text)

Regulated Industries—see also Mass Communication Law, Banking Law

GELLHORN AND PIERCE'S REGU-LATED INDUSTRIES IN A NUT-SHELL, Second Edition, 389 pages, 1987. Softcover. (Text)

Remedies

DOBBS' HORNBOOK ON REME-DIES, 1067 pages, 1973. (Text)

DOBBYN'S INJUNCTIONS IN A NUTSHELL, 264 pages, 1974. Softcover. (Text)

FRIEDMAN'S CONTRACT REME-DIES IN A NUTSHELL, 323 pages, 1981. Softcover. (Text)

MCCORMICK'S HORNBOOK ON DAMAGES, 811 pages, 1935. (Text)

O'CONNELL'S REMEDIES IN A NUTSHELL, Second Edition, 320 pages, 1985. Softcover. (Text)

Sea, Law of

SOHN AND GUSTAFSON'S THE LAW OF THE SEA IN A NUT-SHELL, 264 pages, 1984. Soft-cover. (Text)

Securities Regulation

HAZEN'S HORNBOOK ON THE LAW OF SECURITIES REGULA-TION, Second Edition, Student Edition, approximately 1000

Securities Regulation—Continued

pages, 1990. (Text)

RATNER'S SECURITIES REGULATION IN A NUTSHELL, Third Edition, 316 pages, 1988. Softcover. (Text)

Social Legislation

HOOD, HARDY AND LEWIS' WORKERS' COMPENSATION AND EMPLOYEE PROTECTION LAWS IN A NUTSHELL, Second Edition, 361 pages, 1990. Softcover. (Text)

LAFRANCE'S WELFARE LAW: STRUCTURE AND ENTITLEMENT IN A NUTSHELL, 455 pages, 1979. Softcover. (Text)

Sports Law

SCHUBERT, SMITH AND TRENTADUE'S SPORTS LAW, 395 pages, 1986. (Text)

Tax Practice and Procedure

MORGAN'S TAX PROCEDURE AND TAX FRAUD IN A NUTSHELL, Approximately 382 pages, 1990. Softcover. (Text)

Taxation—Corporate

WEIDENBRUCH AND BURKE'S FEDERAL INCOME TAXATION OF CORPORATIONS AND STOCKHOLDERS IN A NUTSHELL, Third Edition, 309 pages, 1989. Softcover. (Text)

Taxation—Estate & Gift—see also Estate Planning, Trusts and Estates

MCNULTY'S FEDERAL ESTATE AND GIFT TAXATION IN A NUTSHELL, Fourth Edition, 496 pages, 1989. Softcover. (Text)

Taxation—Individual

HUDSON AND LIND'S BLACK LETTER ON FEDERAL INCOME TAXATION, Third Edition, approximately 390 pages, 1990. Softcover. (Review)

MCNULTY'S FEDERAL INCOME TAXATION OF INDIVIDUALS IN A NUTSHELL, Fourth Edition, 503 pages, 1988. Softcover. (Text)

POSIN'S HORNBOOK ON FEDERAL INCOME TAXATION, Student Edition, 491 pages, 1983, with 1989 pocket part. (Text)

ROSE AND CHOMMIE'S HORNBOOK ON FEDERAL INCOME TAXATION, Third Edition, 923 pages, 1988, with 1989 pocket part. (Text)

Taxation—International

DOERNBERG'S INTERNATIONAL TAXATION IN A NUTSHELL, 325 pages, 1989. Softcover. (Text)

Advisory Board

HISTORICAL INTRODUCTION TO ANGLO–AMERICAN LAW

IN A NUTSHELL

Third Edition

By

FREDERICK G. KEMPIN, Jr.
Member of the Pennsylvania Bar
Emeritus Professor of Legal Studies
The Wharton School
University of Pennsylvania

ST. PAUL, MINN.
WEST PUBLISHING CO.
1990

COPYRIGHT © 1973 WEST PUBLISHING CO.
COPYRIGHT © 1990 By WEST PUBLISHING CO.
                    50 West Kellogg Boulevard
                    P.O. Box 64526
                    St. Paul, MN 55164–0526

Library of Congress Cataloging-in-Publication Data

Kempin, Frederick G.
   Historical introduction to Anglo-American law in a nutshell / by
Frederick G. Kempin, Jr. — 3rd ed.
      p.   cm. — (Nutshell series)
   Includes index.
   ISBN 0–314–74708–7 : $12.95 (est.)
   1. Law—Great Britain—History and criticism. 2. Law—United
States—History and criticism. I. Title. II. Series.
KD532.Z9K44   1990
349.42—dc20
[344.2]   90–36979
                                                                CIP

ISBN 0–314–74708–7

Kempin, Anglo-Amer.Law 3rd Ed. NS

PREFACE TO THE THIRD EDITION

This book is about the history of Anglo-American Law. It tells a continued story of the development of its institutions: courts, juries, judges, and lawyers; the sources of law: custom, cases, legislation, and doctrinal writings; and traces the beginnings and development of selected legal concepts: property in land, liability for injury, contract, negotiability of commercial paper, and the business corporation.

An acquaintance with legal history is valuable in three areas: first, as a part of general cultural history, for law is a significant part of all cultures; second, as an aid to the understanding, criticism, and assessment of the current state of the law; third, as an integrating medium in the understanding of economic, social, and political history, for each of these affects, and is affected by, the law.

Legal history can dispel many commonly held misconceptions. One is that the common law is held in the iron bands of tradition through the doctrine of precedent. But precedent is little more than comparing present cases with past cases. Assuming it could happen, were precedent slavishly followed, law could not change except by statute.

Case law does change. There is scarcely a legal rule today that does not have its opposite at some time in legal history.

Precedent, experience, and tradition provide a basis for stability but are also the starting points for change. Successive cases provide opportunities for subtle changes in the meaning of words, unnoticed alterations of approaches to analysis, and minute development of concepts. Sometimes gradually, sometimes suddenly, it is realized that a new legal idea has come into being.

The history of our law is a history of change. Without the need for violent social revolution, the common law has adapted to changes in our social and economic structure from feudalism through mercantilism to a modern capitalistic society. In deciding disputes between individuals it is inevitably concerned with conflicting theories of liability and of the enforceability of agreements. It has assisted in conquering royal absolutism. It denies uncontrolled discretion to individual judges. It oversees the world of business, and directs business to place the public interest above profit.

Not all of this was done by judges. From time to time legislative prodding was needed for the law to respond to new conditions. From time to time the common law's balance between stability and change, tradition and experiment, did not provide the conceptual basis for legal change. This is also part of legal history.

In law, as in other areas of human activity and learning, three valid questions may be asked: where did it come from, where is it, and where is it going. Where the law came from can be traced through legal history; where it is now can partly be explained by legal history; where it is going may be indicated by trends and enduring principles revealed by the study of legal history. It is the task of legal history to refresh the social recollection and to add criticism and analysis to basic historical information.

This book was written to provide an introduction to Anglo-American legal history. In a happy conjunction of the policy of the West Nutshell series and my desires, there are neither footnotes nor endnotes. The reader can be assured, however, that all factual statements have been verified. The book has no bibliography. I believe that it would be much too long if it completely reflected all the sources used that I remember or have on file and, even were it short, most of the important references are highly technical.

This book's predecessor was a set of materials prepared in 1959 for use in a course on Legal Institutions at the University of Pennsylvania's Wharton School. In 1963 the first edition was published by Prentice-Hall, Inc., titled *Legal History: Law and Social Change*, as one volume in its Foundations of Law in a Business Society series.

Each volume in that series was limited to 120 pages.

After a mutually pleasant decade of association, in 1973 the second edition was published by West Publishing Company as part of its Nutshell series, a series which permitted more than doubling the number of pages. This enabled me to include more expository material in the hope of fostering clarity and understanding, more material on policy, competing interests, and the interrelationship of law and other aspects of society, and to introduce new subject matter.

In the years since 1973 new insights have been developed by researchers on some of the topics of this book, particularly torts and contracts. These changes alone made a new edition necessary. Essential additions, changes, and deletions were also made in other chapters, based on the author's reading and research. The chapters on the courts, the jury, and the legal profession were extensively altered, but only the negotiable instruments chapter was left relatively untouched.

I express my sincere thanks and appreciation to readers of prior editions whose interest has made this new edition feasible, and to those who have, personally, by letter, and in print, given me the benefit of their comments and criticisms. I am encouraged to hope that this new, revised, and enlarged edition will serve even better to advance the basic purpose of fostering interest in Anglo-

American legal history among lawyers, educators, students, and the public, in this country and abroad.

FREDERICK G. KEMPIN, JR.

May, 1990

*

OUTLINE

PART I. THE BACKGROUND OF THE COMMON LAW

PART III. THE COMMON LAW IN ACTION

PART IV. THE COMMON LAW CODIFIED

OUTLINE

*

TABLE OF CASES

References are to Pages

HISTORICAL INTRODUCTION TO ANGLO–AMERICAN LAW

IN A NUTSHELL

Third Edition

*

PART I

THE BACKGROUND OF THE COMMON LAW

CHAPTER I

WHAT LEGAL HISTORY IS ABOUT

The law—as was said with resignation of the poor—is always with us. Some twenty centuries before the Christian Era, Hammurabi promulgated his famous code for Babylonia. The Mosaic code of the Israelites is only eight centuries younger. Even before those ancient codes, practices and customs were the equivalent of law, if not true law in the modern sense, among primitive people. Some primitive societies in our own day are still controlled by such amorphous law.

Every legal rule, idea, or norm had its own genesis. All started somewhere and had some cause. Some came about by chance, and thought gave birth to others. Some stemmed from one man's weakness; others were the fruit of strength. Some still echo with the noise of ancient struggles; while passing time and change of custom formed some others.

1

Today, as ever, law pervades our lives. This is its nature, because law guides our relations with each other. It tells us how we may be punished for our crimes; it makes us pay when, by our fault or not, we injure others; it says what we must do if we want our promises to be enforced as contracts; it makes us pay our taxes; it requires us to take out licenses in order to engage in business, to get married, and even to practice such a pastoral pastime as the art of angling.

Every mature system of law has a long history from its inception as a system, back through its archaic and almost forgotten predecessors, to its remote origin in its primitive-law background. Our Anglo–American system of law has been relatively mature (in the sense that it has been the object of study by a separate legal profession) for the past eight hundred years. It was preceded by the archaic and almost lost legal system of the Anglo–Saxons and finds its remote origins in the laws of the Germanic tribes which settled England in the middle of the first millennium.

Most modern Anglo–American legal concepts have been developed in the past eight hundred years. A few may stem from Anglo–Saxon times, but it would take considerable imagination to find precursors of modern law in the primitive Germanic system. On the other hand, our law has not been developed in isolation from the law of the rest of the Western world. No little debt is owed to

Roman law, and the canon law of the Church has contributed its share of ideas.

A realistic point in time to begin a discussion of Anglo–American legal history, then, is with the common law as it stood when it first became the object of study by a distinct legal profession, though excursions into the time before, and into other systems, will be necessary to explain particular points. This initial date is the beginning of the thirteenth century.

WHAT IS MEANT BY LEGAL HISTORY

The question, what is meant by history in general is a vexed one, and difficult to answer. The meaning of the history of law is equally troublesome. In all history we have the questions of when, where and why certain events occurred. In addition we have the develcpment of thought concerning those events.

Take the case of war. We want to know when certain wars were fought, where they began and why they occurred. Our own Civil War, for instance, has been studied for over a hundred years, and there are those who have followed virtually every major engagement and skirmish and can tell us who was where at what time and how the event turned out. This is a painstaking and exacting task. In addition, students of the art of war have theories on why certain battles were lost and which strategies and tactics were successful or unsuccessful and why. From the facts they have spun theories. Others have been concerned with the causes of the total conflict—social, political, economic, philosophical, physical and behavioral.

The history of law is similar. Instead of battles we have cases and legislation, themselves the outcome of struggles between competing persons and groups. Study of these struggles has resulted in theories concerning their causes and effects.

In legal history, as in general history, the first efforts were directed toward finding out what occurred. The next was to try to ascertain why they happened. Conclusions on the first problem are always subject to being upset by new findings of sources. Conclusions on the second are also insecure, as knowledge in those fields which assist interpretation widens. The accuracy of the first step can to some extent be measured by objective standards of historical scholarship. As we employ, however, methods and approaches of modern social and physical science unknown to those who brought the events about, speculation and subjectivity necessarily increase. All too often there are insufficient data available to arrive at a provable conclusion, and sometimes none at all.

Most legal thought has been developed anonymously in the processes and procedures of the courtroom and the legislative chamber. It has been institutionally, not individually, developed. Sometimes individual thought has been adopted as part of law. Political and, of recent years, economic and sociological thought are examples. Much of our current constitutional law was originally developed by individuals and then adopted by the framers or judicial interpreters of our constitutions. Our antitrust statutes recognize economic thinking, and our approaches to the problems of race relations reflect to some extent sociological thought, and the thought of the behavioral sciences in general. Legal philosophy, more accurately called jurisprudence, at times has found its way into judicial and legislative determinations. Jurisprudence in itself is not law; it is the thought of individuals about law and what the law should be.

By legal history, then, we mean at minimum the development of the concepts, doctrines, and rules which have been used to keep order in our society. They arose at particular times out of particular circumstances and, to the extent possible, should be examined and interpreted in the light of those times and circumstances. At best, therefore, legal history should tell us why things happened. Sometimes we know, sometimes we speculate, and sometimes we just have no idea.

Although social conditions, constantly changing, are the context within which law develops, it cannot validly be claimed that they are solely responsible for legal change. Ever since the legal profession developed, the thinking of lawyers about the law has been the main source of change. In some historical periods lawyers' thinking about law was, it seems, totally isolated from social conditions. Thinking about law was sometimes nothing more than a game for its own sake, and law so devised often developed as theoretically logical derivations from accepted legal propositions.

Social conditions affect statutes, which are usually enacted in the hope of curing some apparent evil or providing some remedy. Lawyers are not necessarily dominant in the legislative process. The thinking of lawyers, however, does affect the way statutes are interpreted. In the process of judicial interpretation the law may be led a long way from the original "intention" of the legislators and interpretation may result, in effect, in a new statute. This has been true from early to the most modern statutes. Lawyers, in private litigation and in suits that involve a branch of government, may press for interpretations that narrow or expand the scope of the statute. Judges, within the bounds of precedent and basic legal theory, must choose. Whichever party prevails, the law changes. The same process occurs in litigation based on established principles of the common law. Lawyers describe this process with the aphorism that "The law changes with its application."

THE PRE–NORMAN SCENE

The early thirteenth century lawyers whose efforts were to culminate in the creation of a new legal system, the common law, were the products of the Norman Conquest. Descendants of the Scandinavian conquerors of western France, the Normans were administrators. They brought little written law with them to England, but they transformed existing Anglo–Saxon law. Their faculty for administration developed the Norman courts and legislative bodies whose processes created our earliest body of law.

The Norman conquerors of 1066 did not enter a virgin wilderness, and they did not conquer savages. They conquered a country with a fairly well-defined system of government, including law and courts of law. William the Conqueror purported to enter as legitimate occupant of the throne, and one of his first acts was to promise that the law would be enforced as it was in King Edward's (the Confessor's) time (1043–1066). In truth, the Norman law was not radically dissimilar in concept or in practice from Anglo–Saxon law. In administration the Normans were far ahead of their English subjects; but in law no such clear advantage existed.

The basic values of pre-Norman English society were those common to all Germanic nations. The relationship between a vassal and his lord was primary. The follower owed his lord protection during life and the avengement of his wrongful death. A similar obligation made it necessary for a man to take vengeance or to obtain compensation when a member of his family was killed. The rules of blood feuds were closely regulated by law and custom: in the type of vengeance that might be taken, in the amount of compensation that might be exacted, in the place at which the compensation should be paid, and in the circumstances under which compensation need not be paid. If an outlaw was killed, no vengeance could be taken by his kin, and the same exemption applied to one who killed another while defending his lord or a close female relative. The influence of the Church on the side of compensation instead of physical vengeance tended to temper the violence of the times, but the blood feud survived until after the Conquest, with varying degrees of strength, in all parts of England.

Pre–Norman government was decentralized. Shires (counties) had long been the basic units of government, some of them having been the domains of the Germanic conquerors who came five centuries before the Normans. A sheriff, an ealdorman, and the bishop governed the shires, with little assistance or hindrance from the royal government. There was, indeed, a king, but he usually governed in concert with a council of wise men called the *witan*, frequently convened by the weaker kings, and not at all by some of the stronger ones. In either case, the king's power was not great, and his kingship was not hereditary, because the witan had the right to elect his successor. Alfred, for instance, became king on the death of his brother, to the exclusion of his brother's sons, who were minors.

Each county was divided into administrative units called hundreds, roughly parallel to our townships or parishes, and responsible only to the county. The smallest units were the vills, settlements in which ordinary folk lived.

And last, there were the boroughs, large and small, usually fortified in Anglo–Saxon days. When trade grew and new modes of warfare demanded walled castles, boroughs became locations for fairs and markets.

CHANGES EFFECTED BY THE NORMANS

The Norman conquerors made certain changes in administration which, although they were to have radical effects, did not greatly alter existing English customs. Instead of the indeterminate Anglo–Saxon witan, composed of such important men as the king chose or felt compelled to call into assembly, the Normans created the Great Council or Magna Curia. It was headed by the king and composed of the lords to whom he had given extensive tracts of land as a reward for their faithfulness, and the great ecclesiastics who, as part of their duties, also held church land. From the Curia the House of Lords ultimately developed, and added to it was what became the House of Commons. These are obvious models for American bicameral legislatures.

The Norman kings obtained control of the shires or counties simply by appointing the county sheriffs. That office ceased to be hereditary and became subject to the close control of the king and his administrative officers in the Exchequer (finan-

cial office). The palatine counties in the north and
west were exceptions because they were military
buffers against the Welsh and Scots, and in return
they were granted virtual independence. As part
of the price for papal approval of the Conquest, the
bishop was removed from the administration of the
shires and separate Courts Christian were established for ecclesiastical matters. These measures
accomplished two goals: the Church was removed,
as it wished, from secular affairs, and ecclesiastical
matters were reserved to the Church without interference from lay persons.

The ealdorman, whose position in Anglo–Saxon
society is hazy at best, disappeared.

In administration, the Norman kings used personal confidants who were charged with specific
duties, sometimes judicial, sometimes ambassadori-
al, sometimes purely administrative. These officials, who might perform many different types of
tasks during their careers, constituted the lesser
council, or household, and together with the great
council were part of the King's Court, or Curia
Regis.

In Anglo–Saxon times, a loose lord-vassal relationship had existed. A person who held a large
tract of land had in his entourage a number of
thanes who originally were warriors. Each thane
was entrusted with a tract of land, usually not
transferable to his heirs, from which, by using the
labor of the villeins, he could support himself. The
Normans, however, exchanged this for an adapta-

tion of Continental feudalism. Feudalism was a system of landholding based on a personal relationship. In return for an oath of homage, the king granted vast tracts of land to privileged chief lords, on condition that certain services should perpetually be rendered to him. In essence, the king was purchasing the services of the lords. Instead of money, which was rare in an essentially unmoneyed economy, he paid the lord by giving him the use of land from which the lord could support himself. These lords could then grant portions of their land to other lesser lords, in return for an oath of homage or fealty, again on condition of perpetual services. The system was military in its inception, for the highest type of feudal relationship was based on the tenant's giving military service to his overlord. Other changes the Normans made included removing land cases from the hundred to the county (shire) courts. There, under the sheriff's administration, disputes over land ownership could be decided in accordance with royal policy. Duke William also abolished slavery and the death penalty, but the latter was reinstated by his son two decades later. A more subtle change was the introduction of French as the spoken language of the law.

ANGLO–SAXON AND EARLY NORMAN LAW

Anglo–Saxon law was custom and custom was law. There was neither a legal profession in the form of lawyers and judges nor a body of technical legal knowledge. A few Anglo–Saxon kings reduced the custom of their areas to writings, called *dooms*, that set down the penalties for wrongful acts.

Because of these written dooms, we know something about their criminal law, if we can call it that. Listed crimes were those of violence and disloyalty: treason, homicide, wounding, assault, rape, and theft. For treason, the punishment was death. For homicide, compensation might be paid unless it was accomplished by poison or from ambush. For a killing in an open fight, a sum (*bot*) was paid, part of which (the *wer*) went to the king, and the remainder (the *wite*) to the kin of the deceased. A scale of compensation for lesser injuries fixed a higher rate for important persons, churchmen, and nuns than for the general population. Theft, in Anglo–Saxon times, might result in slavery not only for the thief but his family. If caught in the act or fleeing with the loot, a thief could be killed. The ideas of imprisonment as a punishment for crime, or as a place for the convicted person to be penitent, or in which to reform, were unknown. The jail was merely a place in which to hold accused persons until trial. Penalties varied among different areas in England. Rape, for instance, was punishable by death in some areas and by money payment in others.

Because there was little commerce, there was little commercial law. Its content is to some extent conjectural. Contract in the modern sense was unknown, and sales took place by delivery of the article sold. If delivery was to be made in the future, it was secured by a deposit or by a pledge (*wed*) which would be forfeited for nondelivery. Promises under oath were not uncommon, and their breach put one within the jurisdiction of the Church.

There was little ownership of land as we know it, that is, in the form of an interest which can be sold or willed to one's heirs. Some lands given by a written charter from the king and witan might be devised by wills, but these were uncommon.

PRELIMINARY DEFINITIONS

The law, in common with other areas of learning, has specialized meanings for certain words and phrases. Since recurrent use will be made of some of these terms, the most usual of them will be explained, preliminarily, at this point.

The Common Law and the Civil Law

The term "common law" refers to the system of law developed in England and transferred to most of the English-speaking world. It is distinguished from the civil-law system used in Continental Europe and in the areas of other continents conquered and ruled by Continental nations. Some independent nations, such as Japan, chose independently to adopt some form of the civil law system.

Many ancient systems of law, such as the Egyptian, Babylonian, and Greek, have totally disap-

peared. Others, such as the Hindu, Japanese, and
Chinese, have been incorporated in some measure
into modern systems. Of non-Western systems
that survive, the Mohammedan is the most important: Islamic law is based on the Koran, as interpreted by tradition and juristic writings. Islamic
nations that separate law from religion, however,
tend to follow non-Islamic models.

The civil-law system can be traced back to Roman law, which for Roman citizens extended to the
limits of the Empire. With the disintegration of
Rome, its law lost its universality. Wherever it
was applied, it received admixtures of local customs and differed in content in various parts of
Europe. Civil law received its modern impetus
from the early nineteenth-century French codes of
law created by French jurists under the direct
leadership of Napoleon Bonaparte. The common
law, however, is purely a product of English constitutional development.

The basic distinction between the two systems
lies in the sources of law on which they rely. The
common-law system considers prior decided cases
to be very high sources of authority. The doctrine
of *stare decisis* (let the decision stand) in one of its
forms is the essence of the common-law system.
That doctrine states that courts should adhere to
the law as set forth in prior cases decided by the
highest court of a given jurisdiction as long as the
principle derived from those cases is logically essential to their decision, is reasonable, and is ap-

propriate to contemporary circumstances. Different courts apply this general policy with varying degrees of strictness; English courts, for instance, are inclined to be more rigorous than American courts in its application.

The civil law, however, is oriented toward a legislative code of laws, a comprehensive enactment of all the basic law of the country. When a controversy is presented to a court or lawyer, the immediate problem is to find the appropriate code provision covering the situation and then to apply it to the problem at hand. The courts look to the writings of scholars to aid them in interpreting code provisions. Cases are not ignored, but they do not have anything approaching binding authority on judges.

Statutes in Common–Law Jurisdictions

Common-law jurisdictions, of course, rely on statutes as well as on court decisions. Modern legislatures have vastly enlarged the role of statutes, so that they cover a large proportion of legal problems. Some of the United States even compile their statutes into what are called codes. In addition, particular segments of the law are "codified" in all jurisdictions, so that there are criminal codes, negotiable instruments statutes, sales statutes, and, lately, the Uniform Commercial Code, which covers a broad spectrum of commercial law.

The common-law courts have, in common with civil-law courts, the right to interpret statutes, but the rules of statutory interpretation are many and difficult to apply. In the United States the general policy is to attempt to interpret a statute in the light of the intention of the legislature. In England, however, courts have often held that a statute should be read without reference to legislative intent.

Constitutionality

The courts of the United States, together with those of West Germany and Australia, go one step further. They can declare a statute to be invalid because it conflicts with their written constitutions. This is true not only of the Supreme Court and lower federal courts of the United States, which can declare both state and federal statutes void for contravening the Constitution of the United States, but also of state courts, which can declare state statutes void for contravention of the state or federal constitutions.

Judicial review of legislation is foreign to most civil-law countries. Consequently, their legislatures make the ultimate decision as to the constitutional propriety of legislation. West Germany is a notable exception, and Brazil, Burma, and Japan have a degree of judicial review. France, since 1958, has had a Constitutional Council with some power in that connection, but the council is not part of the French judicial system.

England has no written constitution, but its form of government under an amalgam of customs and ancient statutes, which are its "unwritten" constitution, is no less definite and certain than our own. The pivot of English government is the cabinet system, which is purely customary and does not depend on statutory authority. Restraints on government are essential elements of English government, and that part of our written constitution which we call the Bill of Rights has its English counterpart in many of its particulars.

It is the considered opinion of the English courts that no court in England may declare a statute void on the ground that it is unconstitutional. This does not keep English courts from exercising control over statutes, however. Through the device of interpretation, for instance, any court, whether in the civil- or the common-law system, can keep statutes in line with generally accepted principles and can even, on occasion, entirely emasculate a statute.

Civil Law Distinguished From Criminal Law

Within a legal system the term "civil law" is used to distinguish private actions from public wrongs, which fall under the heading of criminal law. When one person, organization, corporation, or branch of government sues another to obtain a remedy for a supposed injury, the case is a civil case, leading to a possible remedy in money damages or an order to do or not to do a certain act. When the state prosecutes an individual or corporation for breach of a rule of conduct set up by the legislature, the case is a criminal case, which may result in a fine or imprisonment.

The same transaction may give rise to both a civil and a criminal action. A simple case of assault and battery, for instance, may result in a civil action by the victim to obtain damages for injuries sustained and also in a criminal action by the state to punish the guilty party by fine or imprisonment.

Common Law and Equity

The term "common law" is also used to distinguish one segment of Anglo–American law from another part called "equity." Today the terms refer to different sets of legal doctrines.

For centuries the English legal system had two types of courts existing side by side. The older of the two was known as the common-law courts. Another set of courts, including the Courts of Chancery and Star Chamber, developed those principles we now call equitable.

Basically, the courts applying equitable principles acted when the common-law courts either would not act or reached results that were so strict and technical as to be unjust. The net result of their activities was the creation of a set of principles to be applied when the common law did not provide a suitable remedy for a particular wrong. It is still basic theory that one cannot obtain an equitable remedy if an adequate legal remedy is available.

Equity has both substantive and procedural aspects. Suppose the question arises of the enforcement of a trust—an arrangement by which one person or corporation is entrusted with property to manage for the benefit of another person. This question will be subject to the law of equity. It was in the old English Court of Chancery that the law of trusts developed, at a time when the common law courts did not enforce them.

Suppose that a vendor (seller) of a house backs out on the deal. The vendee (buyer) may sue for damages under common law principles, but if he wants a court to force the seller to sell (specific performance) he uses principles developed in equity.

Some American jurisdictions, such as the federal and New York, have abolished the distinction between courts of law and equity and administer both types in the same court. A few, such as New Jersey, retain entirely separate courts of equity and law. Others, such as Pennsylvania, have a judge sit alternately as a common law judge and as an equity judge.

The distinction is anachronistic, but even where law and equity courts have been merged the principles must be kept separate. The reason for this is that all our Constitutions guarantee jury trial in civil cases only in cases under common law principles. Juries were not used in the old English Court of Chancery, and are not used today in a case involving the application of equitable principles. Either the abolition of the jury in civil cases, or its extension to equity cases, would be needed in order for the distinction between law and equity to be unnecessary. Neither step is likely in the immediate future.

Definition of a Court

The word "court" has been used in many senses. It derives from the Latin word *curia* and was originally used to refer to the rectangular enclosed yard of a medieval house. It came to refer to a group of persons either formally or informally gathered together, and so we speak, for instance, of a reception at the Queen's Court. The early English royal councils were referred to as *curiae* or courts. Since the earliest justices were members of the King's Council, they were part of his court. This meaning of the word as an assembly of persons is still used in Massachusetts, where the legislature is called the General Court. The early English law courts, composed of a number of "suitors," were called courts because they were groups of persons. When a single judge came to preside over the proceedings, the word "court" was applied to him or to the place at which he presided. When the office of judge became separated from the King's Council and attained a position of constitutional independence, the term continued in use.

Trial and Appellate Courts

Every modern court system has both trial and appellate courts. The trial courts are courts of first instance and have two functions: to determine the facts and to apply the applicable law to those facts. Appellate courts, on the other hand, have only one function: to determine whether the trial court applied the correct law.

A trial court consists, usually, of one judge who presides over the trial and rules on questions including the adequacy of the lawyers' written pleadings, the admissibility of evidence, and the law in the case. If there is a jury, it decides what the facts were, on the basis of the evidence presented, and usually applies the law to those facts in accordance with the judge's charge. If there is no jury, the judge both decides the facts and applies the law.

An appellate court consists of three or more judges. If it finds that the trial court erred, it may, in appropriate circumstances, either grant a new trial or reverse the trial court's verdict without a new trial. For instance, if it believes the trial judge erroneously admitted or excluded testimony or incorrectly charged the jury, it may order a new trial. If there was no jury and if there is no question about the judge's conclusion of facts or about the admissibility of evidence, but only the question of whether the judge of the trial court applied the correct law, the appellate court may simply reverse the lower court and grant judgment for the other party.

CHAPTER II

THE COURTS

Because the law developed out of the processes of the courts and legislatures, with the assistance of the legal profession, we must carefully examine the origins and processes of these institutions. The form of an organization and the substance of its activities are indissolubly intertwined. What, for instance, would become of baseball if there were only two bases? We might have cricket. Or what would become of corporate management if proxies were once again made illegal? How would congressional committees perform if seniority were removed as a basis for chairmanship? How many Supreme Court decisions on constitutional issues would stand if Congress, by statute, could overrule them? This interrelationship of form and substance gives primary importance to a discussion of the emergence of courts, juries, and the legal profession. In many cases, the development of law was closely affected by the organizational structure of those institutions at the time the concept, doctrine, or rule had its origin.

Today we say that the judge determines the law; this has been true for the past seven hundred years. But until long after the Conquest, judges were unknown. There were "courts," but they were composed of lay persons called suitors, who answered questions of "law" on the basis of their knowledge of local customs. The heads of these bodies—the reeves, sheriffs, lords, and stewards— merely presided. Law was not yet a specialized body of knowledge that needed professional judges.

ANCIENT COURTS

Before royal justice dispensing a common law could come into being (i.e., a law uniform throughout the kingdom), it had to displace the existing system of courts. These courts, at the time of the Conquest, were the communal courts of the shire and hundred, the seignorial courts, and the borough courts.

Hundred and Shire Courts

Composed of suitors who were required to attend as a condition of their land holdings, the hundred court was presided over by the hundred reeve. Some hundred courts were purchased by lords with the consent of the king and council, and these lords could exclude the sheriff. These were called "courts leet." The reason was economic: the lord would receive one-third of any recoveries, in addition to various fees.

After the Conquest the jurisdiction of the hundred courts over land disputes was removed to the shire courts, and they also lost any jurisdiction they may have had over criminal cases. The retained jurisdiction over other disputes of ordinary citizens.

The hundred courts, however, continued to be important as the first step in the criminal justice system. In a day without police, apprehending a person accused of a crime but not caught red-handed was a problem. A process called "frank-pledge" was developed from an Anglo–Saxon predecessor. Families were divided into "tithings," which were groups of about ten families. Tithings were responsible for producing members of the tithing that were accused of crime. The sheriff, or the lords of courts leet, would appear at the large semi-annual meetings of the hundred court and make sure that all inhabitants of the hundred were in a tithing. This was called "view of frank-pledge." Those accused of smaller crimes would be tried on the spot, and those accused of major offenses would be held over for the shire court.

The shire courts, by definition, covered a territory that encompassed numerous hundreds. Its suitors and litigants were the more important persons in the shire. They were courts of general civil and criminal jurisdiction. The hey-day of the shire courts was the first century after the Conquest.

In order to strengthen the administration of the criminal law, a statute, the Assize of Clarendon, was promulgated in 1166. It required twelve men from each vill and four from each hundred to come to the large semi-annual meetings of the shire court and report on offenses committed in their hundreds and produce the offenders, if possible. If the offender was not produced, the shire court would issue a summons, and if the accused did not appear after five consecutive summonses he could be declared an "outlaw." An outlaw had no rights, and was outside the protection of the law.

By the same 1166 statute, jurisdiction over the most important criminal cases, known as Pleas of the Crown, was taken from the shire courts and given to the emerging royal courts. Shire court jurisdiction over land disputes was also taken from them during the reign of Henry II (1154–1189) and assumed by the royal courts. Both developments were part of the centralization of English government in the hands of the royal government at Westminster.

The shire courts retained jurisdiction over many civil disputes as well as lesser crimes. The decline in prestige of the shire courts, however, can be seen in the practice, starting in 1236, of permitting its suitors, who had been important men, to send attorneys to the shire courts in their stead. In the late 13th century the rule arose that the shire courts could not hear cases for amounts over forty shillings. The inevitable reduction in the value of money due to inflation over the years meant that the shire courts ultimately could hear only the smallest claims.

Seignorial Courts

The seignorial courts were not so ancient as the communal courts, but were in existence at the time of the Conquest. They were based on the concept that lords had the right and duty to hold court for their underlings.

Under the form of feudalism introduced by William the Conqueror, each royal grantee of land could grant portions of it to junior tenant lords, and so on down the feudal ladder to the lord who ultimately, through his villeins, worked the land. This process was known as subinfeudation. One who granted land to another was known as the "tenant in service," because he did not actually use the land but was only entitled to services from his tenant. The one who ultimately worked the land, through his villeins, was known as the tenant in demesne.

Each tenant in service had the right and duty to hold court for his junior tenants. This court, composed of all the tenants, decided their disputes and could be asked to advise the lord on problems of mutual concern. The greatest of the seignorial courts was the court of the king, who was at the top of the feudal pyramid. It was known as the Curia Regis. Courts in the intermediate rungs of the feudal ladder were known as Honors, or Courts Baron, and in these courts a tenant in chief (one who held his land directly under the king), for example, would meet with the barons who held land under him to obtain their advice and preside over the resolution of their disputes.

The manorial court for the tenants or villeins on the land was the court of the tenant in demesne. Courts for villeins had the lord or his steward for a judge; those with jurisdiction over freemen however, had the lord or his steward for presiding officer and freemen as suitors.

The powers of manorial courts varied according to the customs of the manor. Some had the right to fix prices of basic commodities made and sold on the manor—an important right, since the manor was a relatively self-sufficient economic unit, producing its own food and clothing. All could try civil actions between tenants or villeins, and had some criminal jurisdiction, which varied in extent from manor to manor.

The administrative functions of manorial courts, which included the allocation of services to be rendered to the lord by the various tenants, continued well into the eighteenth century, and records of copyhold estates in land were kept on the manors until 1925, when an act of Parliament modernized the law.

Borough Courts

The boroughs had their own courts in which the citizens of the boroughs, the burgesses, were the suitors. These courts did not have criminal jurisdiction. If a person within a borough owned land under a lord, he also owed suit to the court of that lord.

The boroughs were centers of trade and commerce and were particularly adept in branches of the law that involved those activities. The royal law, when it finally came into being, was intended primarily for a landed aristocracy concerned mainly with problems of real estate; the borough law might be said to have reflected bourgeois problems. Borough courts were in part responsible for the development of commercial law, since many of the disputes that came before them involved merchants and artisans.

Borough courts resisted encroachments of royal jurisdiction for centuries and were still a potent force at the time the American colonies were founded. Indeed, some authorities maintain that borough law was the law most familiar to many of our influential early settlers, and that early American law contained a heavy admixture of borough law.

BEGINNINGS OF THE ROYAL COURTS

The king's Magna Curia, or Great Council, was the most majestic of English courts. It consisted of all the tenants in chief, other magnates, and great ecclesiastics. The king's personal advisers also met with it. This Great Council performed a multitude of duties, which were not separated into the modern classifications of executive, legislative, and judicial. It advised the king on matters of state, decided cases between the tenants in chief, accomplished accords between Church and state, and acted as a type of legislature.

When the king's personal advisers met alone they constituted another distinct court known as the Lesser Curia, or Household. From the members of this body the king chose justices to take care of his affairs throughout the realm, including the dispensing of justice, particularly criminal justice. The king's justices were particularly important in the close supervision of the shires. They saw to the collection of taxes by the sheriffs, to the punishment of those who were guilty of offenses included within the ever-expanding list of Pleas of the Crown, and when they visited the shire courts they superseded the sheriff as presiding officer. It should not be forgotten that for almost four hundred years after the Conquest, the king of England was also duke of large areas of France, and his justices journeyed there as well.

With the passage of time, additional specialized duties were given these personal representatives of the king. There were Justices of Gaol Delivery, who tried smaller criminal cases; traveling Commissioners of Oyer and Terminer (to hear and decide) who decided important criminal cases, and, until the fourteenth century, the General Eyre of the Justices in Eyre, which made penetrating investigations into all aspects of shire administration.

From 1195 onward, the Crown appointed local citizens to aid in the administration of justice. They were organized by the Statute of Winchester (1285) and, in general, had the duty of keeping custody of indicted prisoners until the king's justices arrived to try them. Permanent appointment commenced in 1327. In 1344, in conjunction with other persons in the county who were "learned in the law," they were given the power to try prisoners for felonies and breaches of the peace. In 1368 they were empowered to try some prisoners by themselves. It was around this time that they acquired the title of justice of the peace.

In this country the modern substitute for justices of the peace are the small claims courts. Until recently, the justices of the peace were not, in many states, required to be lawyers. In addition to their jurisdiction over small claims they have jurisdiction over minor misdemeanors such as traffic law violations. In states that have retained the grand jury, they are also the first step in the criminal justice process. Persons accused of crimes and apprehended are first brought before these lower judicial officers to determine whether there is sufficient evidence to hold the accused for a grand jury hearing.

REFORMS OF HENRY II AND ORIGINS OF CENTRAL COURTS

In the reign of Henry II (1154–1189) there began a series of events that ultimately resulted in a system of royal courts and a law common to all of England. The movement started with an implementation of the royal claim to ownership of all the land in England.

Before discussing the royal courts, a short explanation of the writ system is needed. To start a civil lawsuit today, one may merely file papers in a court of competent jurisdiction. The initial plaintiff's paper is called a "Statement of Claim," a "Complaint," or similar title. A copy is served on the defendant in one way or another.

In the twelfth century, however, one first had to obtain, in effect, the consent of Council to bring suit. One had to purchase a writ (which is nothing but a letter) from the Chancellor's office addressed to the court in question. The writ ordered the court to hear the case. Council determined the types of writs that could be issued, and the king and Council were faced with the fact that any attempt to remove the administration of justice from communal (local) and seignorial courts would be departing from tradition. Therefore movement toward central administration of justice was gradual, and was directed toward cases in which the central government had a strong interest. Chief among these were land cases, because land was virtually the sole source of wealth.

The king's court had always had power to decide land cases involving tenants in chief, who held directly of the Crown. Disputes between lesser lords were decided in the court of the lord of whom the land was held and who was tenant in service over it. Early in the twelfth century the king began to interfere with this jurisdiction by a decree stating that the lord's court could hear a case involving important interests in land only if a "writ of right" had been directed to him by the king. This writ, or letter, from the king directed

the lord to do justice between the plaintiff, who
demanded the land, and the defendant who was in
possession, and stated that if this were not done
the king would hear the case (indeed, he usually
did). Later, on the fiction that the lord had sur-
rendered to the king his right to hold court, the
writ was issued directly to the defendant, thus
bypassing the lord's court and bringing land cases
directly into the royal courts.

The involved nature of the proceedings under
this writ, the delays that could be interposed, the
primitive mode of proof, and the fact that the
decision could be contested by third parties if they
acted within a year and a day—all this made the
writ of right something less than an ideal remedy.

In 1166 Henry II devised the first of a new series
of writs called the possessory assizes. They were
designed to remedy the defects in the writ of right.
The first writ, called *Novel Disseisin* (newly dispossessed), directed the sheriff of the county in which
the land lay to gather twelve men of the neighbor-
hood to determine whether the person on the land
had, in fact, wrongfully taken it from the plaintiff,
as alleged. The issue raised was dispossession, not
ownership. If it was determined that the defendant had dispossessed the plaintiff, he was required to return the land, and if he still claimed to
be the true owner, he, in turn, had to bring a writ
of right. This procedure finally disposed of most
cases. Other types of the writ also were developed.

The Court of Common Pleas

The possessory assizes proved so popular that the King's Council could not take care of all the cases brought. In 1178 five justices were appointed from the king's retinue to hear them. These justices were subservient to the Council and reported to it, but their position differed from that of other king's justices in that they had a continuing commission and did not operate on an *ad hoc* basis. Their conclusions were reported in Council, and in theory the Council made the actual decision.

In the century following 1178, this court, first called the "bench," gradually freed itself of subservience to the Council. In 1234 it started to keep its own records, and in 1272 it was given a chief justice. After Magna Carta (1215) its location was fixed at Westminster. In the third decade of the thirteenth century it acquired its final name, the Court of Common Pleas.

In addition to its jurisdiction over land cases, the Common Pleas soon acquired jurisdiction over other civil disputes such as actions to enforce obligations under a sealed instrument by the writ of covenant and actions to enforce payment of the agreed price of goods sold and delivered by the writ of debt. The court, of course, did not invent these writs. They were issued by the chancellor on the authority of the Council.

The Court of King's Bench

Other cases were heard by the King in Council. For instance, those important criminal matters called Pleas of the Crown were still in his hands. These too, however, were delegated to permanent bodies as they became more numerous and time-consuming.

The body to which criminal cases were delegated was called, in its full name, "The Justices Assigned for the holding of Pleas before the King Himself." Its common name is King's Bench. In theory the king, but actually the assigned justices, decided its cases. This court was so much a part of the King's Council that noble members of the Council attended some of its sessions. By the reign of Edward I (1272–1307) it was sufficiently disengaged from the Council to be recognized as a separate court.

This court exercised power over the king's other officials through the writ *quo warranto,* which asked "by what authority" they held a certain office or did a certain act. Power over other courts was exercised by writs of prohibition, mandamus, and certiorari. Writs of prohibition ordered another court to cease its consideration of a case. A writ of mandamus ordered a public official or body to perform an act or restore a privilege. The writ of certiorari ordered another court to send up its record for review. Writs of error and bills of exception were developed for the purpose of reviewing Common Pleas errors on the record.

The power of King's Bench to review cases decided in Common Pleas derived from the fact that Common Pleas decisions had been subject to review by the full Council at the time when King's Bench was still an integral part of it. When judicial duties were delegated to King's Bench, the power to review Common Pleas decisions was among them; and when King's Bench finally separated fully from the Council, this jurisdiction continued. The errors reviewed were primarily technical or procedural, and the review was not the equivalent of a modern appeal.

At its inception, King's Bench was a criminal court and a court of review over civil cases from Common Pleas. Most criminal acts, particularly those of a violent type, also involve civil aspects. If one, for instance, commits assault and battery, he is likely to be prosecuted criminally and to pay a fine or go to jail if found guilty. He is also subject to a civil suit for money damages by his victim. King's Bench had jurisdiction over the criminal aspect of such cases and, at the instance of the injured party, came by the reign of Edward I (1272–1307) to extend its jurisdiction to the civil side of the case. It took jurisdiction over the defendant because he had committed a breach of the king's peace, then dropped the criminal aspect and tried the civil suit.

Exchequer of Pleas

The Court of Exchequer of Pleas was the third of the common-law courts. The Exchequer was the treasury of the king. As part of its function it had, necessarily, to decide legal questions of tax liability to the Crown.

In addition it developed, around 1326, the famous procedure of the writ *quo minus,* which may have arisen in this way: A person was hailed before the Exchequer to answer a claim for taxes. He alleged that he would be glad to pay, but that he could not pay because John Doe owed him money and refused to pay him. Then the Exchequer would call John Doe before it to find out whether he actually owed the Crown's debtor the money. If he did, the Exchequer would order John Doe to pay.

It did not take ingenious minds long to discover that this was an ideal way to collect a debt. By using the Court of Exchequer of Pleas, the plaintiff had the full power of the Crown behind him. The obligation of John Doe, if found to be due, was owed to the court itself; therefore, the plaintiff did not have to follow the usual modes of execution on a judgment, but could have the Crown collect the money for him. The allegation that the plaintiff owed the Crown money became entirely fictitious and nontraversable (could not be denied). From this humble beginning, Exchequer of Pleas expanded its jurisdiction into complete civil coverage, a process which was completed by 1579. It also had certain equity functions which were not merged with those of the Court of Chancery until 1842.

The Court of Chancery—Equity

The courts of Common Pleas, King's Bench, and Exchequer of Pleas developed the bulk of civil and criminal law. In part, this occurred by the invention of new writs, but much change came about through the stretching of existing concepts.

By the fifteenth century the system of law created by these courts was highly developed. Various circumstances combined, however, to slow down the process of further legal development and growth. Disturbed political conditions and internecine warfare made invention of new remedies inappropriate. The weight of the law itself gave rise to a disinclination to change. The common-law courts were created for a landed aristocracy, and the development of trade and commerce created needs for new remedies and ideas that were difficult to fit into the older remedies and theories based on land law.

In any event, appeals for extraordinary remedies were directed to the king and Council. This body, in accordance with usual administrative practice, referred certain matters to one of its members for action, and that member was the chancellor, the most important member of the Council. The chancellor, before 1474, heard appeals for extraordinary remedies and related his recommendations back to the Council for final action. Sometimes he was instructed how to dispose of a case, but more often he made suggestions to the Council.

As a delegate of the Council, the chancellor enjoyed unusual powers. He could, for instance, issue the writ of subpoena which ordered parties to appear before him under penalty of imprisonment for refusal. In addition, he was not bound by the technical rules of pleading and procedure of the common-law courts. The Court of Chancery never had a jury. The chancellor could delegate his duty to hear cases to masters appointed by him, subject always to his review. Owing to its relative informality, to its background as a court of extraordinary relief, and to the clerical background of pre-Reformation chancellors, Chancery justice was likely to be more flexible than the technical justice afforded by the common-law courts. The separate principles it developed became known as equitable rather than legal.

By 1474 Chancery had become a separate court. Its wide jurisdiction continued. Since its primary mission was to grant relief unobtainable in common-law courts because of a deficiency there of either theory or remedy, conflict with those courts was inevitable. In the first place, Chancery created new fields of law in areas left open by the common law, such as the enforcement of trusts, the law of fraud, and relief against penalty clauses in contracts. Second, it created new remedies such as specific performance and injunctions. And third, it took upon itself more direct interference with common-law processes. On request of a petitioner who was being sued in a common-law court, for example, Chancery might order a litigant not to proceed in the common-law court. On occasion it would take a case already decided in the common-law courts and decide it anew, with the decision often going the other way. In such cases it would issue a writ of prohibition against the party who had won in the common-law court, forbidding him to proceed on the basis of that court's decision. These claims to supremacy were vindicated in the early seventeenth century by a royal commission. Although political considerations probably entered the commission's deliberations, the position taken doubtless was historically valid as far as Chancery's right to give extraordinary relief was concerned.

Because the chancellor was a Crown official, his office supported the claims of James I (1603–1625) and Charles I (1625–1649) to prerogative powers, that is, the claim that all governmental power stemmed from the king and, therefore, that Parliament and the common-law courts were subsidiary to him. Parliament, of course, opposed these claims. This struggle reached its climax and resulted in the execution of Charles I in 1649 and the abolition of the monarchy. For a time Parliament theoretically reigned supreme in a so-called Commonwealth period followed, in 1654, by a Protectorate headed by Oliver Cromwell, who held the title of Lord Protector but in fact, although not in theory, held dictatorial powers. Cromwell died in 1658, and virtual anarchy ensued until the restoration of the monarchy with the recall of the son of the executed king, who was crowned as Charles II in 1660. During the Commonwealth period, Chancery went into eclipse, to regain its power only with the Restoration.

During the eighteenth and early nineteenth centuries, Chancery's rigidity in procedure and technicality in substance rivaled and even surpassed that of the common-law courts. In addition, the fact that it had only one chief officer, the chancellor, who might be asked to review any case decided by the masters in Chancery, made it intolerably slow. Final reform of Chancery procedure did not occur until the middle of the nineteenth century.

Proceedings in Chancery were begun by a bill, which differed from a writ in two significant ways. First, it had no set form and could be simply a general request for relief. Second, it issued directly from the court and did not require the approval of any other body. The bill device was also used in some of the cases before King's Bench.

Star Chamber

The last of the major courts created before the parliamentary revolution of the seventeenth century was the Star Chamber. Its origin is uncertain, but it appears to have been the remnant of the medieval King's Council after the separation of Chancery from that body. The House of Lords had grown out of the Magna Curia long before 1474, and the House of Commons had been in existence for at least a century and a half by that time. Under Henry VII (1485–1509), the first of the Tudors, two acts were passed that either conferred or recognized Star Chamber's jurisdiction. The title Star Chamber came, apparently, from the name of the room in which the court sat. After the creation of the Privy Council to assist in executive matters in the 1530's, Star Chamber became purely a court. It dealt with matters involving magnates who might defy the regular courts, and with matters that threatened the security of the realm, such as criminal libel, conspiracy, forgery, and, later, fraud and the punishment of judges.

In its inception, Star Chamber was, in a true sense, a court of equity. That is, it granted, on principles of natural justice, remedies unavailable elsewhere. But its seventeenth century association with the king's prerogative, its application to criminal and political cases of equity's traditional broad and unchecked discretion, its use of torture to obtain evidence, and its often inhumane penalties made its later reputation somewhat less than enviable. It finally was abolished by Parliament in 1641 in the course of the disputes between Parliament and Charles I preliminary to the military revolution. With its passing, the original jurisdiction of the King's Council over legal matters disappeared. Star Chamber's jurisdiction passed into the hands of the other courts.

Church Courts

Until the Reformation, the church courts exercised jurisdiction over offenses against religion and morals, matrimonial matters, and the chattels of deceased persons. By the time of the Reformation their criminal jurisdiction had disappeared, and after that period their jurisdiction over decedents' personal property passed to the Court of Chancery.

The High Court of Parliament

Basically the House of Lords sitting to try cases, the High Court of Parliament entertained proceedings in error from the King's Bench. The High Court's authority was based on the theory that the jurisdiction over errors of the King's council was inherited by the House of Lords when it became distinct from the Council. Appeals from the Exchequer of Pleas went first, theoretically, to an Exchequer Chamber created in 1357, and appeals from this body were heard by the High Court of Parliament. It was not clear until the seventeenth century, however, that this court could hear appeals from Chancery.

Magna Carta stated that one was entitled to the judgment of his peers, and it referred, in part, to the right of peers of the realm to be tried by the King's Council. When the High Court of Parliament fell heir to the remnant of the Council's judicial authority, jurisdiction over the felonies and treasons of peers of the realm was a part of the inheritance, until the right was abolished by statute in 1948.

Conclusion

Our sketch of court development describes, essentially, a separation of the duties of government.
The ancient King's Council was concerned with the
totality of governmental affairs. Separation of the
House of Lords and the addition of the House of
Commons deleted its legislative function. Delegation of judicial duties to the courts of Common
Pleas, King's Bench, and Exchequer of Pleas took
away substantial judicial function, and much of the
remainder was lodged in the chancellor when he
became head of a separate court. Vestiges of judicial power remained in Star Chamber; but with its
abolition, the judicial power of the medieval Council disappeared. The later Privy Council, product
of a new theory of government, had no judicial
power in England. It did, however, have judicial
power to review decisions made by colonial courts,
and therein lay the basis for conflict between the
colonies and the mother country.

By the time of the political theorists of the
eighteenth century, the English constitutional system was well secure. That system, and not pure
theoretical speculation, provided the basis for the
separation of powers doctrine. The contribution of
the theorists was to rationalize and provide a theoretical framework for that which already existed,
and in the process to refine it into a new framework of government.

MODERN ENGLISH COURTS

The Judicature Act of 1873 consolidated a series of statutes, redrafted in the Supreme Court of Judicature (Consolidation) Act of 1925, and overturned the whole classical structure of the English courts. Modern England has a Court of Appeals with two divisions, one for civil and one for criminal cases, often presided over by the same judge.

AMERICAN COLONIAL COURTS

It was against the background of the English system that the American colonies and states created their own court structures. Neither their system of courts nor their law was adopted totally from the mother country, but they had no other experience to draw on. They were lower- and middle-class people whose day in court might have been on the manor or in the borough, and they knew little of the niceties of pleading and practice in the royal courts. Colonial law was not permitted to controvert the laws of England, but its proceedings attested to the fact that there was more law in England than that administered by the royal courts.

The colonies did not have a common system of court organization. Some colonies were royal, others were proprietary, and others were modeled after the joint stock trading companies. The colonies were differently settled—some by a fairly homogeneous community of religious dissidents, others by those who sought new opportunities to garner wealth, and yet other groups contained a fair proportion of the criminal element sent over to rid England of their presence.

Although generalities are impossible for the thirteen colonies over the period of 175 years they were subject to England, a few observations can be made. English practice was followed in many ways. For instance, the colonies retained the local judiciary known as justices of the peace, or magistrates. In many colonies, justices of the peace sat a few times each year as minor criminal courts known as Courts of Quarter Sessions. As in England, they were not required to be learned in the law.

Terminology followed English usage in some places. Pennsylvania used and uses the term "Court of Common Pleas" for its civil trial courts, and Pennsylvania's and Virginia's major criminal courts were called Courts of Oyer and Terminer.

The ancient function of the king and his Council as the highest court was reproduced in many colonies by giving that function to the governor and his Council. A peculiarity of the colonial system, in addition, was that the Privy Council in England heard appeals from judgments of the highest courts of many colonies.

On the other hand, colonial conditions caused many changes from English practice. Separate courts of equity or Chancery were late developments, and early colonial courts administered equity and law side by side in the same courts. Simplicity was also demonstrated by the colonial treatment of procedure and evidence, in which— from a combination of lack of training and distaste for the refined technicalities of English practice— elasticity replaced rigidity and substance tended to conquer form.

By the nineteenth century, however, the growth of a better-trained bar brought with it a return to more complicated forms of law and procedure. The importation of English law books, from Littleton to Blackstone, accelerated this process. But some judicial opinions observe that despite the respect in which earlier judges are held, their inadequate learning makes their judgments entitled to little weight. Some of the legislatures in the newer western colonies so deeply deplored the trend to follow English law that they forbade the citation of English cases in their courts. The urge to examine English law for relevant precedents was, however, impossible to resist during the formative period of our own law. There was no other example, realistically, to follow, and the dominant feeling of the times was that law was something more than the opinion of the judges—that there was some general common law which all courts should follow and which, therefore, might well be found in English cases.

By the middle of the nineteenth century, the preconditions of a separate and distinct jurisprudence had been met: sufficient American precedents had developed, texts had been written, and lawyers had been trained. Although English law continued to be searched for precedents where American law was lacking, those areas became fewer and fewer as the years went by.

CHAPTER III

THE JURY, AND OTHER MEANS OF FINDING FACTS

What happened? That is a crucial question in all cases. If the parties agree on the facts, the judge can apply the law and give a judgment. If, however, the parties disagree on the facts, the method of finding facts that has been developed by the legal system must be used.

Today, in this country, facts are found either by a jury or by the judge. In some cases a jury is not available. Examples include lesser crimes known as misdemeanors that involve fines or short prison sentences, actions before administrative bodies, and, generally, actions in that branch of our law known as "equity." In criminal cases the defendant may almost always waive a jury and ask the judge to find the facts. In civil cases the judge will decide the facts if both parties agree to that mode of trial. Whether decided by a judge or jury, wrong conclusions may be reached. No system has ever been developed that is wholly free from possible errors.

To follow the historical development of fact-finding in our legal system, we must consider civil cases and criminal cases separately. Ultimately the jury was adopted in both, but not until the 16th century.

WAGER OF LAW

In the medieval period, and dating back before the Conquest, a common method of fact-finding in civil cases was "wager of law," also known as "compurgation" or canonical purgation, particularly in the church courts. In a case of a suit for money due, for instance, the defendant might in effect deny the debt and offer to wage his law. If the court agreed, the defendant was ordered to return to the court, take an oath that the debt was not due, and be accompanied by eleven "oath-helpers," or some other number as decided by the court. The oath-helpers were not witnesses; they did not need to know anything about the transaction in question. They swore on the Bible that the defendant was a teller of the truth and that his oath was good. If they all so swore, defendant won immediately.

This may seem a curious method of proof, but in small communities, where everyone knew everyone else, it must have been difficult to get eleven people to swear that the defendant was oath-worthy if that was not true. To swear falsely was a spiritual offence, and the result could be excommunication. Excommunication meant, in addition to its spiritual sanctions, that no one could deal with or assist that person in any way. The fear of that penalty was real.

Even as the population grew, and as persons willing to lie on behalf of friends, or for money, became more common and judges refused to order wager of law, it was still preferred by the commercial community, a close-knit group. In suits for debts, for instance, merchants thought it proper for defendants who denied indebtedness based on the evidence of the plaintiff's books to support their denials by wager of law. In London, merchants obtained a statute in 1364 that retained wager of law in commercial disputes. The Exchequer court, which had used the jury, replaced it by wager of law in 1376 at the instance of the legislature. Although it was outmoded by new procedural processes in the 16th century, wager of law was not formally abolished in England until 1833.

For the century after the Conquest, and later in some areas such as the city of London, wager of law was also used in criminal cases. However, it was reserved for cases in which proof was not possible and for defendants who were considered oath-worthy. It could not be used, for instance, by a person found in possession of stolen goods, or by persons in servile classes whose lords could vouch for them. The Crown was not in favor of wager of law in criminal cases. The Assize of Clarendon, in 1166, provided that persons cleared of a criminal charge by wager of law must, if they were considered by lawful men to be of bad reputation, leave the country and cross the sea within eight days unless detained by bad weather. They could not come back to England without permission; if they did, they were considered outlaws.

TRIAL BY BATTLE

Trial by battle was a Norman importation. It was used in two types of cases: private accusations of felony, and contested titles to land.

A private accusation of felony, called an "appeal of felony," was a personal accusation that the other party had committed a felony that involved him or his family, such as robbery or murder. It was not an official indictment. The battle between the two was judicially supervised. Battle was not available when the accused was a woman, was aged or infirm, or when the court could be convinced that the accusation was made out of hate and spite (*de odia et atia*).

When title to land was contested (there were no recorded deeds in those days) the battle was not between the parties but between hired "champions." Each champion would swear that his father, on his deathbed, told him that the land belonged to his patron. Again under judicial supervision, battle would ensue until one party cried "craven" or until the stars appeared. If it was a draw, the defendant was the victor.

Civil trial by battle in land cases was superceded as a practical matter by new court actions that developed in 1166 and thereafter. Appeals of felony disappeared because of lack of use. When, after centuries of disuse, trial by battle was demanded in 1819 it was promptly abolished by the legislature.

THE JURY

Cursed, reviled, blessed, or praised, the jury has stood firm for seven hundred years. So firmly did our forefathers uphold the jury that we find the right to jury trial anchored in our federal and state Constitutions.

There are two types of juries. The first, the "petit jury," is used in both criminal and civil cases. In criminal cases its task is to determine punishable guilt, and it usually does so with little criticism. Its position as a bulwark of liberty, a protector against executive oppression, and as a mode of lessening the rigors of overly strict legislation is secure. A defendant in a criminal case may waive the right to jury trial and rely on the judge. Waiver is common in England, but not in the United States.

The civil jury's task is generally to determine liability to pay money damages. It is noteworthy, however, that the civil jury is not now and never has been used in equity cases, although a few states provide for equity jury trials in very limited circumstances. The reason for the absence of jury trial in equity cases will be given later in this Chapter.

The civil jury is the subject of much criticism. It was virtually abolished in England, its birthplace, over forty years ago. Australia and New Zealand

followed England's lead. The jury has been accused of favoritism toward plaintiffs who sue corporate defendants. It is said to be, in many cases,
incompetent to handle involved testimony, particularly in technical matters. It is often difficult to
determine whether the jury followed the judge's
instructions on the law or whether it followed
"law" of its own making. That is because almost
all verdicts are "general verdicts," that is, the jury
finds for the plaintiff or defendant without comment on why it did so. In this country, nevertheless, accusations of bias, incompetence, capricious-
ness, delay, and expense have gone unheeded.

The civil trial jury, in its defense, has a most
difficult task. It must reconstruct history. It
must determine the facts of a past transaction. If
its verdicts seem excessive one must keep in mind
the impossibility of determining the money value
of such intangibles as pain and suffering or loss of
reputation. Any criticism of the jury must also
take into account possible alternatives. And in
such deliberations it must not be forgotten that
jury verdicts do not create precedents.

The second type of jury is the "grand jury." It
does not decide guilt or innocence; its function is
accusatory. When a possible offender is brought
before a magistrate, and the magistrate believes
there is sufficient evidence, the case is presented to
the grand jury for investigation. Only the prosecution presents evidence to the grand jury. The
grand jury's task is to determine whether the evi-

dence presented, if uncontested, would warrant conviction. If it finds that it does it will issue a true bill of indictment and the case will proceed to trial. If the evidence is insufficient the case will be dismissed.

On occasion a grand jury will be charged by a judge to investigate specific types of possible criminal activity among the general population or among government officials. These investigations may also result in indictment.

The grand jury has been abolished in England and in about one-half of our states. Its continued existence in the federal courts, however, is guaranteed by the Constitution.

Both types of jury fit the classic definition given by Frederick Maitland many years ago: that a jury is a body of neighbors summoned under oath by a public official to answer questions. The trial jury answers the question of guilt or innocence, liability or nonliability; the grand jury determines whether there is enough evidence to warrant a criminal trial. Not only do these juries fit the same definition, but they derive, ultimately and in the distant past, from the same origins.

ORIGINS OF THE JURY

The direct origins of our jury go back over a thousand years to the French empire of the Carolingian kings. Although monarchs in those days did not have to contend with the types of legislatures that later developed, neither did they have the unbridled discretion that in later centuries fell under the heading of divine right of kings. They were, however, subject to custom, which was the prevailing law. Charlemagne, in his successful attempt to unite his empire, used a procedure called the "inquest," or inquisition, to determine the nature and extent of royal rights. He called together the people of the countryside and required them to relate their understanding of the immemorial rights of the king. These rights being ascertained, they were adopted. The importance of this procedure was that it fixed the right of the state to obtain information from its subjects.

Norman Use of the Inquest

The Norman invaders were not long on English soil before they used the inquest, again for royal purposes, in the compilation of Domesday Book, a census of the ownership of all the land in England. It listed landowners, of whom the land was held in accordance with feudal theory, the chattels on the land, and other information. Its purpose was to establish the base for the imposition of taxes and feudal dues. Its name perhaps arose out of popular opinion that the inquiry was as thorough as that to be visited upon men on Doomsday, the Day of Judgment.

For another use of the inquest we must turn to the criminal jurisdiction of the communal courts. Since a person cannot be tried for a crime unless he is first accused, four men from each vill and twelve from each hundred appeared before the county court and voluntarily accused individuals of specific crimes. They were not summoned by a public officer, however, so they did not meet Maitland's definition of a jury.

This voluntary procedure was made compulsory by the Assize of Clarendon of 1166. It was to be called a "presenting jury" and was the predecessor of our modern grand jury.

The Possessory Assizes

In 1166 Henry II instituted the possessory assizes (explained in Chapter II), a new type of procedure for settling disputes concerning land. Land, at that time, was usually transferred by a ceremony called "lievery of seisin." It took place on the land, in sight of witnesses, and involved handing over a symbolic piece of turf or a twig to the new owner, accompanied by appropriate words.

By a century after the Conquest older titles could not be proved by the production of witnesses as they were all dead. Consequently under the writ of right, which was the old procedure to settle land titles, trial was by battle between hired champions. It is said that many monasteries that owned much land were so often in litigation that they had virtual stables of champions waiting for possible suits.

A remedy for this situation was clearly needed. The possessory assizes provided that a plaintiff now had merely to show that he was the last possessor of the land and that he had been *dis-*

seised (dispossessed) by the defendant. There was no need to prove the earliest ownership and there was no battle. The writ directed that an inquest or assize be assembled. This was a group of neighbors who were presumably well enough acquainted with the facts to decide whether a disseisin had in fact taken place. Instead of submitting the crucial question of disseisin to the hazardous fortunes of battle, it was submitted to the persons most likely to know what had happened—the neighbors.

This inquest differed from our jury in that it could not be waived. If the inquest found that the plaintiff had been disseised by the defendant, the defendant was required to restore the plaintiff to possession. The case did not determine which party was the true owner, but merely whether the defendant had disseised the plaintiff. If ownership was still contested the defendant, if he lost, could sue under a writ of right. This, however, rarely occurred.

Around 1179 the defendant was given the option to choose the assize procedure instead of battle under the older writ of right. The plaintiff, however, still had to prove the older title to the land and not mere dispossession.

It is tempting to consider the jury of twelve of the possessory assizes and the newer writ of right as the progenitor of the modern petit jury, but it would be inaccurate. The possessory assizes met a distinct need and were used for some centuries. However, they were superceded in the sixteenth

century by a quicker and less expensive action
called "ejectment." The jury of the possessory
assizes was a predecessor of our petit jury but was
not its source.

The Petit Jury and the Ordeals

For the source of the modern trial or petit jury
we must turn again to the presenting jury instituted by the Assize of Clarendon in 1166. Having
been presented, how were the accused persons to
be tried?

As was seen above in the discussion of wager of
law, some accused persons were absolved on their
oaths, supported by the aid of oath-helpers. Most
people, however, were tried by *ordeal.*

The ordeals were appeals to the supernatural to
determine the guilt or innocence of the accused.
They were called the *Judicium Dei,* judgment of
God, or simply *judicium.* There is some mention
of trial by ordeal in sixth century Frankish
records. The ordeals spread as Christianity spread
to the east in Europe and to England and Ireland.
The greatest use of the ordeals was from the ninth
to the twelfth century. On the continent of Europe, ordeals, in addition to their use in trying
persons accused of crime, were used for political
purposes (e.g., by a claimant to a kingship of land
to prove he was entitled to the land), by women
who were willing to undergo ordeals to disprove
accusations of infidelity, and to determine who

owned certain lands. In England, however, ordeals were used only in criminal cases.

There were four forms of ordeal: hot water (often called the "cauldron"), cold water, hot iron, and morsel. The ordeal of hot water was the oldest. The ordeals of water, cold and hot, were, in the twelfth century, for the poor and the unfree. The ordeal of the hot iron was for lay freemen. The ordeal of the morsel was for clergy accused of crime.

Each ordeal took place as part of a solemn religious service. In the ordeal of cold water, the accused crouched, placed his arms beneath his knees, was bound around his knees and body by a rope, and let down into a pool. If the water received him and he sank he was innocent and was, it is to be hoped, immediately pulled out of the water. In the ordeal of the hot iron the accused held a red-hot iron in his hand, its weight increasing with the severity of the crime, and carried it nine feet. The hand was then bandaged. If after three days the wound was clean the accused was innocent. In the ordeal of the hot water the water was heated to a high heat and the accused was required to plunge his arm into the cauldron and retrieve a stone suspended by a cord. The more severe the crime the deeper the stone was placed, from wrist to elbow depth. In the ordeal of the morsel the accused was required to try to swallow a morsel of bread or cheese, perhaps with a feather imbedded in it. If he could he was innocent, but if he gagged on it he was guilty. Evidence from early cases is said to indicate a preponderance of acquittals.

Despite weighty support by lay authorities from Charlemagne on, criticism of ordeals was expressed as early as the ninth century. By the twelfth century criticism had become general. It was reasoned that ordeals did not necessarily give the correct answer even though the answer came from God. This was based on the idea that the deity may wish to punish an innocent person not for the crime alleged but for some other offense not known to anyone except the accused. Or, the deity may consider the accused to be entitled to another chance.

Churchmen brought forth theological arguments. They noted that the ordeals were non-canonical. They were found neither in the Bible nor in sacred writings. It was also observed that to invoke the judgment of the deity was to tempt God, and that was forbidden.

These arguments were well know in the ninth and tenth centuries but did not prevail because political power was against them. Before the eleventh century the popes of the Roman Catholic Church were basically subject to lay authority. Many popes had been appointed by emperors and some were dismissed by emperors. In 1067 William the Conqueror declared that the king would determine whether a pope should be acknowledged in England. Kings claimed the right to convene synods and councils to change doctrine and ecclesiastical law. Charlemagne convened such a council in year 794, and Duke William claimed that right as well. Bishops and priests were appointed by the king or by feudal lords.

Change commenced with Pope Gregory VII who, in 1075, wrote a revolutionary paper, titled *Dictatus Papae,* which was originally a secret document. He proclaimed the pope's legal supremacy, and that independence of the church from lay authority required power to be centralized in the pope.

In the succeeding centuries the struggle of the church to free itself from domination by the lay authorities led to considerable contention and conflict. In England the conflict came to a head with the murder of Archbishop Thomas Becket. Becket was a friend of Henry II, and was installed by Henry as Chancellor in the belief that Becket would support Henry in conflicts with Rome. To Henry's surprise and chagrin, however, the Archbishop soon declared that he was not responsible to Henry but only to the church and the pope. His murder by four knights at the altar of Canterbury Cathedral in 1170 was believed to have resulted from Henry's expressed desire to be rid of Becket.

Also, during these centuries the canon law of the Roman Catholic Church was developed and put in final form in 1234. It remained unchanged until 1917. Change is quicker today, as the next revision was in 1983. The canon law created a legal system, as distinguished from a legal order.

As an appeal to the judgment of the deity, the ordeals required the participation of a priest. Only after a full mass were the ordeals administered. By the late twelfth century the primacy of the church in matters of faith and practice was well established. The Fourth Lateran Council was convened in 1215, and one part of its work was to accept the criticisms of the ordeals and to forbid priests to take part in them. This was also in line with the continuing effort of the Church to separate itself from the state. This ban, except perhaps for some remote places far from the power of Rome, effectively barred the use of ordeals to determine guilt or innocence.

What alternative remained for the finding of the facts? Let the judge do it? Impossible! He would be replacing the voice of God in the ordeals. After toying with a temporary expedient that imprisoned those of evil repute, banished those guilty of intermediate crimes, and required pledges of security from those accused of lesser offenses, judges began to resort to the presenting juries. At the gatherings of the court were presenting juries from every vill and hundred. Some of them were acquainted with the alleged offense—indeed their members may have been the accusers. What would be more natural than to ask their opinions? A number of jurors, perhaps as many as forty-eight, would be asked whether the accused was guilty or innocent.

They decided, not on the basis of testimony or evidence presented to them, but on the basis of their own knowledge or what they could find out.

Because this procedure was an innovation, the accused could not be required to submit to it. Instead, he was asked whether he would "put himself upon the country," as the saying went. If he refused, his guilt might never be decided, for neither that procedure nor the ordeals could be used.

In an attempt to end the impasse, the Statute of Westminster I (1275) provided that if the accused refused to submit to a jury, he should be put in a strong and fast prison (*prison forte et dure*). A peculiar change in meaning occurred, whereby this phrase came to mean *peine forte et dure,* a legal torture in which the accused was laid on the ground and his chest was loaded with successively heavier weights until he either submitted to trial by jury or expired.

Some accused persons chose to die under this procedure rather than to submit to a jury. Why? If a person knew he was guilty and expected to be convicted by a jury, he would die in either case. It is true that death by judicial execution is quicker than being crushed by weights, but there was another consideration. Conviction of a felony meant that the felon's real property went to the king to a year and a day and then went permanently to the lord of whom the felon held the land. In addition, all of the felon's personal property was forfeited to the king. If, however, the felon died under judicial torture he had not been found guilty and therefore these results would not follow. By choosing this horrible route out of a sure conviction a person could save his family from destitution.

Prisoners were reluctant to submit to the jury because it was composed, in part at least, of the very persons who had accused him. A verdict of guilty, it seems, was assured beforehand. This difficulty was removed, however, in 1351 or 1352, when it was determined that the trial jury should not include any members of the presenting jury that had accused the defendant, if the defendant chose to challenge their presence. The jury, however, still spoke of its own knowledge and did not hear witnesses until about one hundred years later.

Attaint of Jurors and Contempt

Because jurors spoke of their own knowledge until about 1450, it was possible that a jury might knowingly come to a false verdict. A judge who suspected that one had done so could appoint an attainting jury of twenty-four persons to try the members of the first jury for their perjury. If found guilty, they could be imprisoned, and their chattels could be forfeited to the Crown. When jurors ceased to speak of their own knowledge, this procedure became obsolete.

In the sixteenth century, in an attempt to solve the problem of favoritism toward defendants, particularly those accused of political crimes, juries were made amenable to the processes of other courts, including the Star Chamber. In addition, they might be fined heavily for contempt if they refused to follow the instructions of a judge in a criminal case.

Chief Justice Vaughan, in *Bushel's Case* (1670), determined that a jury was not in contempt for refusing to follow such instructions. His reasoning was ingenious. He said that since jurors were already subject to the penalty of attaint for a false verdict, they must be free to come to their own independent conclusions; otherwise they would not be responsible for their verdict. What he said was true in theory because attaint of juries had never been formally abolished, but it was no longer true in fact. By this ingenious reasoning, he succeeded in freeing the jury from political compulsion.

Role of Magna Carta

Even today one is occasionally told that the jury had its origin in Magna Carta, The Great Charter of King John, granted on June 15, 1215, and subsequently reaffirmed by various English kings in revised forms. Chapter 39 said that "No freeman shall be seized, or imprisoned, or dispossessed, or outlawed, or in any way destroyed; nor will we condemn him, nor will we commit him to prison, except by the legal judgment of his peers or by the laws of the land."

This appears to be a guarantee of jury trial. The problem, however, is that there were no criminal juries in England in 1215, the year of the Fourth Lateran Council. The document could only have referred to existing legal institutions.

In those days, and down to 1948, the peers of the English realm were entitled to be tried for crimes by their peers. This meant the Council, and in modern times the House of Lords, and not in the ordinary courts. The reference to dispossession refers, of course, to land. That reference, therefore, was to the jury of the possessory assizes.

Magna Carta, therefore, expressed the historical rights and privileges of the barons who imposed it on King John. To the extent, however, that Magna Carta opposed the unbridled power of the Crown and expressed the rule of law rather than of men, it had an indirect but very real effect on the retention of the jury system. The belief of subsequent generations that Magna Carta was the source of the jury, although incorrect, was extremely important in enabling it to withstand criticism in times of stress.

Extension of the Jury System to Civil Cases

The criminal jurisdiction of the royal courts was based in the court of King's Bench. Common Pleas and Exchequer of Pleas were purely civil courts.

The jurisdiction of King's Bench over crimes was based on their jurisdiction over breaches of the "king's peace." Therefore, in the early thirteenth century, some crimes were not its concern; crimes that did not affect the king and that were tried in the local and seignorial courts. In the latter part of the thirteenth century the criminal jurisdiction of King's Bench expanded to cover more and more crimes.

Then, in the course of the fourteenth and fifteenth centuries, King's Bench developed a jurisdiction over civil actions between individuals that were said to be a breach of the king's peace. Assault and battery is an example. It was an indictable crime, but because it was a breach of the king's peace King's Bench assumed jurisdiction over a claim by the person assaulted for civil damages against the assaulter. Because the jury was the way King's Bench found facts in criminal cases, the jury was also used in their civil cases. These were called actions in "trespass," and today we would call them "torts."

In the meantime, though with less success, Common Pleas used equivalent fictions and subterfuges in civil cases to employ remedies that had been developed in King's Bench. In so doing, it adopted the jury used by King's Bench in these actions. The older actions still relied on wager of law, the ancient method of fact-finding.

The court of Chancery never had the jury. During the centuries that the jury developed and its use expanded in the common law courts, equity was still administered through the king and council. As we saw in Chapter II, Chancery did not become a separate court until after 1474. In addition, its jurisdiction included giving remedies not given by the common law, and these remedies required the exercise of discretion of a type substantially different than in deciding guilt or innocence. Determining, for instance, whether a writ of prohibition should be issued to halt a lawsuit in a common law court is scarcely a proper question for a jury.

THE JURY IN NINETEENTH CENTURY UNITED STATES

Today the role of the jury in the United States is to find the facts and of the judge to find the law. The judge instructs the jury on the law and the jury applies the law to the facts they find. The jury then renders a general verdict. In truth, however, sometimes one cannot know whether the jury correctly applied the law as stated to them by the judge. We can, however, be assured that the law was followed if the judge asks the jury for a "special verdict," that is, a finding of facts to which the judge will apply the law. Special verdicts, however, are not frequent.

At the beginning of the nineteenth century, however, juries decided both facts and law in civil and criminal cases. Part of the reason may be that most colonial judges were lay persons. Formal legal education, except for those few who attended the English Inns of Court, did not exist until late in the eighteenth century. Between 1672 and 1776

Massachusetts had ten chief justices and twenty-three associates, but only one chief justice and two associates were lawyers. Judges were not held in particularly high esteem. The English common law, as handed down by English judges, was not accepted at all in some colonies and even where it was accepted it was carefully examined to see if it met local conditions. John Adams expressed the opinion that "It would be an absurdity for jurors to be required to accept the judges' view of the law against their own opinion, judgment, and conscience." Jurors could ignore the judge's charge on the law, and there are records of the judge and the lawyers for both parties arguing the law to the jury.

By around 1850 the jury's right to find law in civil cases was being denied. The main device used by judges was the "directed verdict." When a judge directs a verdict he really decides the case then and there. The theory is that the facts have been so clearly proved by one side or the other that any contrary answer given by a jury would be arbitrary and capricious. The case does not go to the jury; the term "directed verdict" is a euphemism to conceal the harsh fact that the case is being taken away from the jury and is being decided by the judge alone. The special verdict, explained above, was another way to take away the jury's power to decide the case.

Consequently, today our system of law and fact finding although distinct in theory is a blend in practice. Unless a directed verdict is entered or a special verdict required, the jury gives a general verdict which gives the jury some leeway to depart from the judge's instructions. If, in the opinion of the judge, the jury goes too far off the mark the judge can enter a judgment "notwithstanding the verdict." This cancels the jury's verdict and substitutes the judge's verdict.

The special verdict, directed verdict, and judgment notwithstanding the verdict (referred to as a judgment n.o.v., for *non obstante veredicto*) cannot be used in a criminal trial. They would be denials of due process of law. Therefore in a criminal trial the jury has much more leeway to decide as they think justice requires. Unless a criminal jury engages in unlawful practices, its verdict is final. An appellate court, however, may order a new trial.

Not only did the role of the jury in civil cases diminish during the nineteenth century, but the very institution of jury trial in civil cases came under attack. The competence of the civil jury was doubted, and there were calls for its abolition. Even Oliver Wendell Holmes, Jr., called for a reduction of the jury's role. In discussing the importance of the practical experience of jurors, he stated that "A judge who has long sat * * * ought gradually to acquire a fund of experience which enables him to represent the common sense of the community in ordinary instances far better than the average jury. He should be able to lead and to instruct them in detail, even where he thinks it desirable, on the whole, to take their opinion. *Furthermore, the sphere in which he is able to rule without taking their opinion should be continually growing.*" (Emphasis added.)

One possible reason for the changing position of jury and judge and the degrees of respect accorded to each lies in the external community. Full-time, legally trained, and experienced judges became more and more common. The jury, however, was and is selected from the voting rolls. Over the course of the nineteenth century the voting rolls expanded. Originally consisting only of freeholders, that is, landowners, it gradually expanded to all male citizens regardless of the amount of property they owned. Waves of immigrants from southern and eastern Europe arrived. They did not share the Anglo–American legal experience, were not sensitive to local conditions, and did not know local practices. Naturalization proceedings required only minimal knowledge of our institutions. Disrespect for the jury may well have followed.

PRESENT STATUS OF THE JURY IN THE UNITED STATES

Today the grand jury exists in only half of our states and in the federal judicial system. It was abolished along with the petit jury in England in 1948, and does not exist in civil law countries. The petit jury exists in all our states and in the federal system, except for equity cases, although it is often waived. In civil law countries the petit jury is not used in civil cases, but in some civil law countries a petit jury is occasionally used in criminal cases.

The modern alternative to the grand jury is accusation by information. Informations were used in early England, particularly by the Council and Star Chamber. The district attorney or other appropriate official directly orders the criminal court to try a criminal case. Under the information procedure, prosecution of a criminal case depends on the decision of the district attorney's office.

Conclusion

From this résumé of the evolution of the jury system it should be apparent that there is nothing in its history to require its indefinite continuance. From an instrument of royal oppression it became a means of protection against state interference. But this change was the happenstance of situation and not the product of intrinsic merit or planned growth. For cases in which the jury meets modern needs, it should be continued. For cases in which it does not, it should be eliminated. Whatever substitute may be found for the jury, however, the basic problem of reconstructing the history of a transaction will remain. A more professional technique of fact determination, therefore, may not necessarily result in greater speed, impartiality, wisdom, or truth.

It might be observed that our judicial system does not always have the finding of truth as its primary objective. We note, of recent years, judicial disapproval of various means of ascertaining truth—wire-tapping, drug-induced testimony, entrapment into illegal acts, and the like, each of which is considered an infringement under many circumstances of constitutional rights. Just as science can enable us to ascertain truth with greater, although not absolute, certainty, so it can enable the state to oppress and persecute its citizens. The balance between convicting the guilty and protecting the civil rights of all is not an easy one to establish or to maintain.

CHAPTER IV

THE BENCH AND BAR

Lawyers are a hardy group. Derided by poets, shunned by utopians, suspected by many of the public, they have survived. The lawyer's glory, and his greatest problem, is in his ability through knowledge of the machinery of government and of justice to get things done. When a lawyer submits to occupational temptations, the public is indignant; but all too often they do not know or understand that the lawyer may have erred while trying to assist an importuning client. In a sense a lawyer's friends are dangerous, because in seeking to achieve what he believes to be a fair goal, he may depart from strict adherence to professional ethics. The delicate balance between the lawyer's duty to his client and his duty to his profession is not an easy one to maintain.

The lawyer's position in society appears to vary with his influence and income. It also varies, however, with the types of persons represented, and with the type of law practiced. In general, a prosperous lawyer who represents socially acceptable clients on problems common to such clients has the highest prestige. As his income falls, however, and as his clients become less respectable and their problems aberrations from socially acceptable norms, his status in society is lower.

FUNCTIONS OF LAWYERS

Lawyers survive because people need their two important functions: advice and advocacy. Advising, or counseling, is an informal, often personal, function. The lawyer drafts a will, assists in buying a house, starting a small business, or forming a large corporation. Advocacy is a formal function by which the lawyer represents and speaks for the client—usually before a court or administrative body—but advocacy may include representation in other forms also.

In the United States all lawyers are authorized to perform both functions, counselling and advocacy. Individual lawyers and lawyers in small firms commonly engage in both functions, although they may specialize in the types of cases they will take. The members of large law firms are typically divided into those who are expert in courtroom work, a minority, and the others who specialize in office work.

In England the bar has always been divided into those who perform the advocacy function and those who are counsellors. For the past two hundred years there have been barristers and solicitors. Barristers have a monopoly on the right to appear in the higher courts—Crown courts, High Court, Court of Appeal, and House of Lords. Barristers do not deal directly with lay clients, but only with solicitors.

Modern English barristers are divided into two types: juniors and seniors. The seniors are called Queen's Counsel (QC) or, if a male is on the throne, King's Counsel (KC). They also, because of their gown material, are called "silks." They are effectively appointed by the Lord Chancellor after consultation with others. They constitute about ten percent of the bar.

QCs may not engage in preliminary work, and by practice are assisted by juniors who receive roughly two-thirds of the fee. However, the juniors' portions generally exceed what they would earn if they took the case on their own because QCs charge significantly higher fees than juniors. Judges of the higher courts are selected only from QCs.

Solicitors perform the counselling function and may appear in lesser courts. When a solicitor's case must be heard in a higher court the solicitor engages a barrister. Because the bulk of legal work is counselling, there are many more solicitors than barristers. In 1988 there were about 48,500 solicitors and 5500 barristers.

LAWYERS' FEES

The English barrister's fee is paid by the solicitor. Barristers are not permitted to sue solicitors for their fees, and uncollected fees are a problem. Fees are set by the barristers' clerks. Fees are not competitive and, indeed, the clerks commonly seek the going rate.

In general, in the United States the client pays a fee to the lawyer whether the suit is successful or not. There are numerous exceptions, such as the right of a shareholder who sues the corporate officers in a suit brought on behalf of the corporation to recover reasonable attorneys' fees, and the right of a successful plaintiff in an antitrust suit to recover reasonable attorneys' fees by statute. The rationale of the first is that the money judgment obtained is a benefit the corporation should pay for, and of the second is that the successful suit is a public benefit.

In England, however, in all cases the winner is entitled to reasonable attorneys' fees from the loser. The same is true, with some variations, in western Europe. In England a court official sets the reasonable fee to be paid by the loser. One rationale is that the winning party should not have to pay for enforcing legal rights.

In the United States contingent fees are permitted in many types of civil cases. The lawyer's payment is "contingent" on the client winning. These fees are referred to in television advertisements: "We don't get paid unless you recover." Widely used in accident cases, a contingent fee is a percentage of the recovery that goes to the lawyer for the successful plaintiff, generally one-third but up to half the recovery. If the plaintiff loses the lawyer gets nothing. Contingent fees are forbidden in England and western Europe. Greece permits contingent fees, but with a top limit of 20 percent.

ORIGINS OF THE BAR

The origins of the bar are found in necessity. Until the body of legal knowledge, including procedure, had become too much for the ordinary person to handle there was no need for a legal profession. But by the time of Henry II (1154–1189) it was possible for a litigant to appoint someone to do his technical pleading. This person, the *responsalis,* was not a member of a separate profession, for apparently anyone could act in that capacity. He eventually developed into, or was superseded by, the attorney who was appointed in court and had the power to bind his employer to a plea. By the thirteenth century, attorneys constituted a recognized profession.

Just as technical pleading required the aid of an attorney, so oral argument came to require special skill. The privilege of appearing in person before the king's justices became a hollow and dangerous one as the law became more technical. By the time of Henry III (1216–1272) judges had become professionals, and the courts had started to create a body of substantive legal knowledge as well as technical procedure. The narrators, or pleaders, came into being to speak for litigants in court and to perform the function of advocacy.

The king had need of persons to represent his interests in the courts. In the early fourteenth

century, he appointed sergeants of the king
(*servientes regis*) to take care of his legal business.
When not engaged in the king's business, these
fabled sergeants-at-law were the only persons who
could appear as a lawyer in the Common Pleas
court.

Perhaps the crucial event in the beginning of the
legal profession was an edict issued in 1292 by
Edward I. At that time what passed for a profession was in a sorry state. Legal business had
increased tremendously; yet there were no schools
of the common law, and the universities considered
law too vulgar a subject for scholarly investigation.
Edward's order directed Common Pleas to choose
certain "attorneys and learners" who alone would
be allowed to follow the court and to take part in
court business, and made the legal profession a
monopoly.

The effect of putting the education of lawyers
into the hands of the court cannot be overestimat-
ed. It resulted in the relative isolation of English
lawyers from Continental, Roman, and ecclesiastical influence. Lawyer taught lawyer, and each
learned from the processes of the courts, so that
the law grew by drawing on its own resources and
not by borrowing from others. It became insular.
Whether this was good or bad for the development
of the law is a debatable question, but it did create
a unique system with a minimum of foreign ideas.

Obviously the court itself was no place for the
training of these attorneys and learners. The

court did offer aid in providing an observation post, called the crib, in which students could sit and take notes and from which, occasionally, they might ask questions during the course of the trial.

The Inns of Court

The custom of lawyers living together during terms of court, dating back as far as Magna Carta (1215), gave rise to the unique English institution of the Inns of Court. The first, the Honorable Society of Lincoln's Inn, was given a home in the reign of Edward I (1272–1307). Its preserved records date from 1422. Sometime later, Inner Temple, Middle Temple, and Gray's Inn were established. At more than a dozen of these Inns, lawyers and students lived and were taught the tradition and learning of the common law. The Inns were subject to supervision by the judges and were associated with the Inns of Chancery.

Because the Inns also taught things such as music and dancing, it was not uncommon to find members who did not intend to enter the legal profession. Those who did, however, had a long and arduous training. The entering student, after two years of instruction in elementary law as a member of an Inn of Chancery, was admitted to the Inn of Court to which it was attached. For the next four or five years he was trained first in answering legal questions and second in arguing moot cases. At that point, he became an inner barrister and could look forward to another eight years of training. Only then was he called to the bar as an utter (or outer) barrister and permitted to practice before King's Bench. He might also at this point be chosen as a reader to give lectures to members of the Inn. After more experience he might be chosen a sergeant-at-law and permitted to practice before the oldest of the courts, Common Pleas. Sergeants were not permitted to teach, but received the highest fees. Their order was abolished in 1877.

For a time, inner barristers could act as attorneys, and until the 1500's, when they were expelled, many attorneys were attached to the Inns of Court. If attorneys acted for fees, they were required (by a series of statutes beginning with the order of Edward I in 1292) to be approved by the judges. In the eighteenth century, with the formation of the Society of Gentlemen Practicers in the Courts of Law and Equity, the name "attorney" was dropped in favor of the term "solicitor." That was the solicitors professional society until 1903 when the Law Society came into being.

The Inns of Court ceased to teach law during the English Civil War (1642–1646), and did not begin again until 1846. Legal education was nonexistent in England during those two centuries.

In 1758 William Blackstone was appointed to the Vinerian Chair at Oxford University. Blackstone's famous lectures, and the *Commentaries on the Laws of England* that he produced, were not intended exclusively for future practitioners. In the Introduction to his *Commentaries* he wrote that he

thought " * * * it an undeniable position, that
competent knowledge of the laws of that society, in
which we live, is the proper accomplishment of
every gentleman and scholar; an highly useful, I
had almost said essential, part of liberal and polite
education." The *Commentaries* had tremendous
influence in the colonies, and were studied by
generations of American lawyers and judges. Indeed, until the early 20th century the phrase "to
read Blackstone" meant "to study law." Blackstone left Oxford in 1766 to practice law. No
successor was appointed.

There was some legal education in England during the nineteenth century, but not many students.
Cambridge and Oxford offered law degrees, and
University College London had a law faculty but
students were few in number. Toward the end of
that century some provincial universities taught
law, but mainly to those interested in preparing for
the solicitors' examination.

Formal legal education in England was first required by the Solicitors Act of 1922, set at one year
of formal instruction. This led a number of provincial universities to provide law courses. By the
1980s almost sixty institutions, both universities
and polytechnics, offered law courses.

Preliminarily it should be noted that an English
law degree is taken at the undergraduate level. It
is not a post-graduate law school degree as it is in
the United States. Because one may take other

undergraduate degrees, reference will be made to "law graduates," and "non-law graduates."

Today a budding barrister must first be admitted to one of the four Inns of Court and must dine at the Inn at least 32 times in a period of eight terms. Except for a few "mature" students, since 1975 a university level law degree has been required. The few "mature" students must take a year of legal training and the Part I examination in law. Persons with a law degree are exempt from Part I. All candidates must take the Part II examination in advocacy and drafting. They prepare for this examination by taking a practical course at the Inns of Court School of Law (ICSL) and a year of apprenticeship, called "pupillage," in the chambers of a barrister. The ICSL opened in 1964. It offers courses in preparation for Part II but is not a degree-granting institution.

The Law Society regulates the qualifications for solicitors. The current Training Regulations were adopted in 1987, and amended in 1988. Candidates from England and Wales are in one of four categories: law degree graduates, non-law graduates, non-graduates over the age of 25, and non-graduates under the age of 25.

All candidates must at some point enroll with The Law Society, headquartered in London. Law graduates can become solicitors in three years. During the first year the candidate prepares for the Solicitors' Final Examination by taking one year of study at The Law Society's College of Law or at a polytechnic institute. The subjects in this examination are those encountered by solicitors, such as business organizations, conveyancing, and revenue law, which are not generally a part of a university law degree curriculum. The next two years are spent as an articled clerk (trainee) to a solicitor, or other approved clerkship such as with a local government agency or in a magistrate's court. A majority go with a solicitor.

Non-law graduates must, in addition to the requirements for law graduates, begin by taking a year of study at the schools mentioned to prepare for the Common Professional Examination on six core subjects: Constitutional and Administrative Law, Contracts, Torts, Criminal Law, Land Law, and Trusts. These subjects would have been studied in a law degree program. This is followed by the law degree candidates' requirements.

Mature students who do not hold degrees and are over 25 years of age require five years of preparation. "School leavers" under 25 years of age require six years. Throughout the Training Regulations are provisions for various exemptions, and for special cases such as English barristers and solicitors from Scotland and Northern Ireland.

At one time most solicitors left school at the age of 17 and entered directly into clerkships. Today, however, candidates normally have a university level law degree. Because of the difficulty of establishing a practice, barristers occasionally become disbarred voluntarily so that they can apply to the

Bar Transfer Panel Committee to become solicitors.

AMERICAN LAWYERS

In the New World there never was a time when the profession was divided into solicitors and barristers. The English division was part of a social system which did not exist, at least in its full rigor, in the New World. The small size of the colonies likewise made such a system unnecessary.

Some states, however, had two classes of lawyers: attorneys and counsellors. Only counsellors could practice before the highest court of the state.

Requirements for admission to the bar differed in the various states and at different times. In some states each county court admitted its own lawyers. In other states admission to the bar in one county qualified the lawyer to practice in any county of that state. Sometimes the highest court controlled admission to the bar.

Educational requirements also differed. The states varied from a requirement of seven years of preparation to three years. Some required fewer years for college graduates, or waived the requirement if an examination was passed.

In the middle of the 19th century a few states, on egalitarian principles, eliminated all requirements except for "good moral character." One state, into the 1930's, merely required one to pay an application fee.

Until the 1920's, most prospective lawyers were trained in the offices of established lawyers. For a fee, they were permitted to work as legal clerks. Students read Coke and Blackstone, and editors of various editions added annotations to bring the stated law in line with then current American law. Students would be questioned on their readings by the lawyer.

The earliest law school was that of Judge Tapping Reeve at Litchfield, Connecticut, formed about 1784. The lecture method was used, and the lectures were not published because students could have bought the lectures and have avoided paying tuition. The Litchfield School was highly successful and trained many prominent lawyers from many states. By the 1830s, however, competition from published commentaries, such as those by Chancellor James Kent and Judge Joseph Story, caused a decline in students. The school closed in 1833.

University education in law was not prominent before the Civil War. The first was at William and Mary College, in Virginia, in 1779, and continued until 1861. Some efforts, such as those at the University of Pennsylvania and Columbia College, were transient.

Harvard developed a new model for legal education in 1815 when Isaac Parker, Chief Justice of Massachusetts, was appointed Royall Professor of Law. Harvard did not place law in the university's curriculum. The Law School was separate, and except for courses in Roman law and political science its students' education was entirely professional.

Perhaps because Harvard Law School used lectures and texts, as did lawyers in their offices, it did not attract many students. After the death of Joseph Story, who was its main attraction, in 1845, the school entered a period of decline. The appointment of Christopher Columbus Langdell in 1870 and James Barr Ames in 1873, however, heralded a new era.

Langdell and Ames revolutionized law teaching. Instead of using lectures and texts, they introduced the concept of the casebook. The first was Langdell's "A Selection of Cases on the Law of Contracts," published in 1871. Except for explanatory footnotes, its 1007 pages contained no text but 350 edited cases dating from the 16th century onward. By the end of the 19th century the casebook method of instruction was almost universal in American law schools. Today, cases are used but in compilations known as "cases and materials," in which the materials supplement and often dominate the cases.

Langdell and Ames also altered the concept of who should teach law. Rather than to enlist prominent judges and lawyers as teachers, they saw law teaching as a separate profession. The theory was that taught law is scientific law, not practical law, and that legal science could be better developed by those not in active practice. James Barr Ames never practiced law. The concept of law teaching as a separate profession continues to this day, but without the idea that law is a science. In recent years law teaching has come to be recognized as a separate profession in England as well.

After the Civil War law schools started to be formed at many universities as separate degree-granting institutions. Today, law schools require matriculants to have a bachelor's degree. Admission to the bar requires the candidate to have a degree granted by a law school approved by the state where admission is sought.

Bar examinations varied greatly until the 1930s. In 1931 the National Conference of Bar Examiners was formed for the purpose of improving the quality of examinations and of fostering uniformity. Today the bar examination is uniform in all states, except for a part that stresses the peculiarities of the state, basically legal procedure.

THE BENCH

The mystery of the common-law judges can easily be presented but is much more difficult to explain. It is this: the judges of England started as the king's men, representing his personal interests, and ended as protectors of the citizenry against the king's prerogative. This metamorphosis was not complete until the seventeenth century, and it was a change which profoundly affected Anglo–American law.

There were no true judges outside the royal courts. In the communal and seignorial courts there were only suitors who performed the judicial function but were not professionals because they were neither career men nor specially trained. Even the early justices of the king were not professional judges, because they acted on an *ad hoc* basis.

Earliest Judges

The first true judges emerged with the Common Pleas court at the end of the twelfth century. Their positions were far from secure. Because they were selected from the men immediately serving the king, they were subject to his whim for both appointment and removal. Until the middle of the thirteenth century most of them were in clerical orders, although not necessarily involved with clerical duties. Their ability to hold church office and to receive the proceeds thereof enabled even those in the lowest orders to enter the service of the king, who paid low and often uncertain compensation. Clerical status assumed a certain minimum of education, including the ability to read and write—accomplishments not often shared even by the nobility.

In the church courts, *ad hoc* delegates, who spent most of their time in their own pursuits, were appointed for particular cases. Had the common law adopted that system, the development of a full-time professional judiciary would have been considerably delayed.

The common-law system of choosing judges from the king's favorites worked with a fair degree of efficiency until the reign of Henry III (1216–1272). That reign, however, was marked by another revolt of the barons, more devastating than the rebellion that led to Magna Carta in the immediately prior reign of King John. Simon de Montfort, Earl of Leicester, was successful in reducing Henry III to political impotence after the Battle of Lewes in 1264, and that victory was followed by the creation of a Council of Magnates to rule the realm. This unrest, which began around 1256, ended only with the accession of Edward I (1272–1307).

The unrest had an unfortunate effect on the judiciary. Bracton stopped writing his remarkable law book around 1256, complaining that the judges had so deteriorated in quality that to find good English law he was forced to look back to Pateshull and Raleigh, the judicial masters of the 1220's. In 1289 Edward I found it necessary to purge the judiciary. Scandalous reports were made concerning the judges, involving allegations of corruption, bribery, murder, and other heinous crimes. A special commission was appointed by the King to look into the matter, and many of the charges were sustained. As one result, the Chief Justice of Common Pleas fled the country.

During this time important legal advances had nonetheless taken place. Reform began with the Statute of Marlborough in 1267 and continued through the Statute of Westminster I (1275), the

Statute of Gloucester (1284), and the vast Statute of Westminster II (1285). In total, these statutes constituted a revolution in substantive and procedural law.

During or immediately after this period a practice arose of the utmost importance to Anglo–American law: judges were chosen not from the king's favorites, but from eminent sergeants-at-law. Henceforth practicing lawyers were to be the sole source of the higher judiciary. This meant that a community of interest between the bench and the bar would exist to a closer degree than in any other legal system. When in 1292 legal education was entrusted to the judges, the system became totally inbred. Lawyers taught prospective lawyers, judges were selected from lawyers, and judges supervised legal education. This system proved to have a high degree of resistance to foreign ideas and to purely academic theorizing.

Independence of the Judiciary

The judges selected from the lawyers were still, however, appointed only during the king's pleasure (*durante bene placito*). It was only with the Act of Settlement in 1701 that they came to be appointed for so long as they behaved themselves well (*quamdiu se bene gesserint*). Their salaries became certain at that time, and joint action of both houses of Parliament became necessary in order to remove judges from office.

Between 1455 and 1461 the fratricidal Wars of the Roses took place. The swiftly changing fortunes of battle made impolitic, if not impossible, judicial alignment with any particular faction. As a result, the judiciary remained immune from political interference, and a strong precedent was created for the removal of judges from politics. The risk of such interference, however, again became apparent in connection with Queen Mary's attempt to restore Roman Catholicism (1553–1558).

Lord Coke, during his struggles with James I (1603–1625), laid a further basis for the independence of the judiciary. Two cases decided by that memorable jurist, who at one time or another held nearly every important English legal post, stand as firm precedents for the rule of law and the supremacy of the courts. In *Dr. Bonham's Case,* Lord Coke subjected Parliament to the fundamental principle that "when an Act of Parliament is against Common right and reason, or repugnant, or impossible to be performed, the Common Law will control it and adjudge such Act to be void." In the *Case of Proclamations,* Coke and his brethren on the bench gave their opinion to King James that the king was without power to make law. The result was Coke's elevation to the office of Chief Justice of King's Bench, where his views presumably would not be so detrimental to the interests of the King. He was, however, dismissed from that office in 1616, and ultimately went into politics.

The revolution which ended the reign of James II (1685–1688) formally determined the question of judicial independence for all time. That bloodless conflict ended with the supremacy of Parliament established, and with it the independence of the courts. The Act of Settlement of 1701 recognized an existing fact.

*

PART II

SOURCES OF LAW

CHAPTER V

CUSTOM AND CASES

For a technical body of law to exist, some distinct group of persons, a legal profession, must develop it. Such a profession emerges slowly; and in the beginning of any legal system, law is nothing more or less than the customary rules of the community.

CUSTOM AND LAW

Twelfth-century England was ruled by custom. Each manor, each county, and perhaps even each vill had its own customs. The powers of the royal government were customary also. And custom at that time did not have to be immemorially old to be enforced as law. A custom, it was said, was old if it had existed for ten years, very old if for twenty, and ancient if it was thirty years old. Communities could and did adopt customs wholesale from other communities.

Changes in customs controlling the constitution of government, including the courts, created the legal profession. The separation of the judiciary from the council, the writ system, court procedure, the emergence of barristers and attorneys—all were accomplished as changes in custom. Legislation, in the modern sense, was still in the future.

When the legal profession came into existence, it had either to choose its newly emerging law from the conflicting mass of customs in existence or else to create its own customs. Slowly, custom became what was accepted by the royal courts, not the general population. Custom still ruled at local levels where royal law did not intervene and was enforced in the manors, for instance, until the beginnings of the modern period.

The common law was, therefore, the customs of the royal courts. It was this law that became the object of study by the legal profession. As time passed, lawyers began to view unfavorably the idea that outside custom could change the law. By the 1500's it had become the accepted rule that for a custom of the country to be accepted by the courts it had to be immemorially old; and the date chosen was September 3, 1189, the coronation of Richard I.

One result of this rule was to slow the change from the ancient estate of villeinage to copyhold estates, which resemble a fee. In the 14th century the estates of villeins were subject to the courts of the manor, not the royal courts. The ownership of the villein's land was in his lord, who held the freehold that was the only estate in land then recognized by the royal courts. Essentially, villeins had no rights in their land.

After a series of famines, the Black Death came to England from the continent in 1348. It continued to mid–1350, and other outbreaks followed for the remainder of that century. The result was a drastic decrease in the population. This turned the relationship between lords and villeins upside down. Fields were untended, and laborers were scarce. Previously, land had been scarce and labor plentiful, but now labor was scarce. Villeins left the land to work in the cities, where labor was also scarce. Wages rose dramatically. On the land, the lords had to offer more rights to villeins to keep them on the land or to attract the villeins of other lords. This resulted in the estate called "copyhold."

In the 15th century one result of the resistance of the royal courts to accept custom as law was that they started to require proof that the custom of copyhold on a copyholder's manor was "immemorially old." But, of course, there were no copyholds in England in 1189. For a while equity intervened, but full protection for the copyholder awaited the arrival of Lord Coke as Chief Justice of Common Pleas in the early 17th century.

The ability of the peasantry to hold their own land was a momentous development in English social and legal history. The social revolutions that racked other countries resulting from the monopolization of land and denial of peasants' rights in land did not, except for the abortive Peasants' Revolt of 1381, take place in England. The change was accomplished not by revolution but by means of a slow change in custom that was ultimately recognized by the courts.

Pockets of custom persisted in some parts of England and were enforced in the royal courts. One of the most famous of these is the custom known as borough English, under which land devolved upon the youngest rather than the eldest son. This usage was abolished only in the 1920s.

Custom today has slight effect in case law. Meanings of technical terms in contracts, for instance, are defined by custom, and knowledge of commercial custom can often assist a judge in mercantile cases. It does have a compelling effect on legislation in areas in which prior law has been outrun by events. Commercial custom has forced many changes in statutes, and this will be considered subsequently in the treatment of commercial law.

CASES AS A SOURCE OF LAW

Modern American courts assure the careful reporting and publishing of their decisions. This accurate law-case reporting, however, began only in the nineteenth century. Until the reign of Edward I (1272–1307), there was no single place to look for cases. The law books referred to them, tradition carried them forward, and the plea rolls of the courts contained some information, but the exact wording of the decisions was eternally lost.

The Year Books

In Edward I's reign, the compilation of Year Books began a three-century practice. In their first century, the volumes were extremely informal collections, by year, of informal notes of cases taken by lawyers and students. Year books were not usually organized according to subject matter and had no official approval. They were collected because they were useful to the profession. There was no attempt to include all cases nor all cases in their entirety, and comments dealt with judges' personalities and lawyers' quips as often as with matters of legal substance. These notes of cases obtained from diverse persons had no common form.

In the fifteenth century, the Year Books became more professional and uniform. They were still not official, nor did they report cases as soon as they were decided (some cases might be two or three years old). Their compilation ceased in 1535.

When the Year Books had begun to amass numerous cases, Abridgments appeared. They were compilations, usually condensed, of cases reported in the Year Books but arranged by subject matter, apparently to facilitate study, and many of them were produced by students as so-called commonplace books for practice in abstracting cases and in analysis.

Some Abridgments were printed. The earliest of these is one attributed to Statham, at the very end of the fifteenth century. Later published Abridgments obtained more fame, from Fitzherbert's (1516), down to the twenty-three volumes of Viner's Abridgment, published between 1742 and 1753. It was Viner who endowed Blackstone's chair at Oxford.

Abridgments were organized by subject matter. Thinking by lawyers had traditionally gone along the lines of discussion of specific writs issued by the Chancery. Lawyers thought in terms of the writs of debt, detinue, covenant, trespass, and the like, and not in terms of concepts. As one of the earliest uses of alphabetization or organizing things from A to Z, the old mode of thinking just would not do. Consequently the compilers of abridgments had to use classifying terms for headings which, in turn, provided the opportunity for them and their readers to think about the law in new ways. This mode of thinking became part of legal education when students wrote their own commonplace books. Commonplace books were large folios in which the student would write extracts of cases under various subject matter headings as practice in classification and analysis.

Private Reporters

Immediately after the cessation of the Year Books, individually printed reports appeared. Privately published for individual advantage or profit, they still were not official. Different reports covered the same periods and cases. Dyer's reports, for instance, ran from 1537 to 1582 and were duplicated in part by the reports of Plowden, who covered the years 1550 to 1580.

Reports varied in quality. Some of them were of such low reputation that particular judges forbade them to be cited in court; others were most reliable. Variations often appear in the same case reported by different reporters, giving the researcher considerable difficulty. Cases were usually published long after they were decided; current reports awaited the end of the eighteenth century.

Although England still does not have strictly official reports, the United States began to appoint official reporters at the beginning of the nineteenth century. Apparently, the American practice started with the United States Supreme Court in the early 1800's; the states followed at irregular intervals. All states fell in line by the Civil War. Official reports are the only ones that can be cited with authority in the courts, although copies of them are published by private publishing houses (cases being in the public domain and not the subject of copyright). In recent years some states have abandoned the expensive practice of publishing official reports of appellate court cases and have relied entirely for the promulgation of their opinions on the regional reports published by West Publishing Company.

The Doctrines of Precedent and Stare Decisis

In any developed legal system, cases are a source of law. The question, however, is the relative importance given to them, in comparison with the weight given to statutes and treatises.

The Anglo–American legal system adheres to the doctrine of *stare decisis*. If a judge finds a prior case decided by the highest court of his jurisdiction in which the facts are not distinguishably different, he must follow it if the decision is still in the spirit of the times. The highest court of a given jurisdiction must either follow its own prior decision or overrule it. In England the doctrine was, historically, very strict, for there the highest court, by its own rule, could not overrule its own prior decisions. On July 22, 1966, however, the highest court indicated that, while following the rule of *stare decisis,* they are willing to "depart" from previous decisions "when it appears right to do so."

Lord Gardiner's statement, in announcing the changed English policy, noted the value of *stare decisis* in providing "at least some degree of certainty upon which individuals can rely" but also recognized "that too rigid adherence to precedent may lead to injustice in a particular case and also unduly restrict the proper development of the law." The statement also took note of the retrospective nature of case law and warned of the danger of "disturbing retrospectively the basis on which contracts, settlements of property and fiscal arrangements have been entered into and also the especial need for certainty in the criminal law."

Courts in civil law countries, however, do not follow this doctrine. As code nations, they look primarily to the applicable code of laws and to the writings of jurisprudents explaining the codes. The French have been known to deride the doctrine of *stare decisis* as *la superstition du cas,* but nonetheless French judges are affected, although not in a binding way, by a series of decisions that indicates the nature of their law.

Sometimes the doctrine of *stare decisis* is referred to as the doctrine of precedent, but there is a difference, historically, between the use of precedents and adherence to the doctrine of *stare decisis.*

The idea of looking back to prior cases for guidance is as old as our professional courts. In 1256 Bracton did this but chose to reject some cases as "bad law," while accepting others. Instead of finding law from the cases he illustrated law by the use of cases. During the Middle Ages, in the period of the Year Books, prior cases were also inspected, but scarcely revered. Law was not found in a single case; rather, a group of cases illustrated the true law. Law, in this sense, was the total custom of the courts.

There are at least three reasons why a doctrine of *stare decisis* could not have been developed before the nineteenth century. The first is that the general tenor of thinking was distinctly hostile to the idea that a judge could *make* law. Law was something higher than the pronouncements of any court. A decision was merely evidence of the law—the best evidence, perhaps, but nothing more than that. Only in the second quarter of the nineteenth century, with the positivist jurisprudence of John Austin, did thinking on this matter start to change. Austin's concept of law as a command of the sovereign substituted the theory that the judges *made* law for the prior theory that they merely *declared* the law. Austin's teaching is by no means the end of the tale on that subject, but it created the intellectual climate needed for the doctrine of *stare decisis*.

The second reason is that there was no truly reliable system of reporting cases before the nineteenth century. Assuming a case is law, one must know definitively what it says. The Year Books of the Middle Ages did not purport to be complete, and the individual reports varied in reliability. In England, semiofficial reports did not appear until 1865, although they appeared considerably earlier in the same century in this country.

And last, there was no distinct hierarchy of courts, with one highest court in each jurisdiction, until the late eighteenth century. There must be a single voice to declare the law. In the United States this event occurred earlier than it did in England. The federal Constitution of 1789 provided for a Supreme Court, and the various state constitutions did the same. In England there was no one highest court until 1873.

For these three reasons, there was no firm doctrine of *stare decisis* in the United States before 1800. By 1825 some of the older states had started to stress the binding power of a single prior decision, and by 1850 the doctrine was firmly entrenched.

Early American cases reflect the idea that the common law was something more than merely prior cases. Harris and M'Henry, who compiled a series of early cases from lawyer's notes and files throughout the State of Maryland, stated in the introduction to their work that "the foundation of Land Law in this state was laid during the provincial Government. Its leading principles were then settled, partly by the decisions of Courts, and partly by the understanding of eminent lawyers, whose opinions, in many instances, decided and were acquiesced in and received as the law of the land." Illustrative of the force of opinions of eminent lawyers is the 1772 Maryland case of *Nicholson v. Sligh.* According to Harris and M'Henry's reports, it appeared, "from the notes of T. Jenings, Esq., who was counsel in this cause, and of W. Cooke, Esq., that the Justices present being at a loss to determine the points, desired that the opinions of some of the gentlemen of the bar not engaged in the case, might be taken; and thereupon the whole matter was referred to James Hollyday and

Thomas Johnson, Esquires" whose opinion was taken as the law by the court.

A 1786 Pennsylvania case, *Kerlin's Lessee v. Bull,* also expressed the idea that the law was something more than cases. The opinion there stated that "A court is not bound to give a like judgment, which had been given by a former court, unless they are of opinion that the first judgment was according to law; for any court may err; and if a judge conceives, that a judgment given by a former court is erroneous, he ought not in conscience to give the like judgment, he being sworn to judge according to law."

By the 1850's, however, both Maryland and Pennsylvania had switched to a position of firm adherence to precedent. Other eastern states followed the same general trend toward strict adherence to *stare decisis.* Perhaps the most remarkable statute ever passed on this question was adopted by the State of Georgia in 1858. The statute stated that decisions of the Supreme Court of Georgia are law if three judges have concurred, and "shall not be reversed, overruled or changed; but the same are hereby declared to be, and shall be considered, regarded and observed by all the Courts of this State as the law of this State, where they have not been changed by the legislative enactment, as fully, and to have the same effect, as if the same had been enacted in terms by the General Assembly."

In part at least the difference between the traditional English and American attitudes toward *stare decisis* can be explained on the basis of our colonial status—a love-hate relationship at times. It is clear that early American courts were unwilling automatically to apply English precedents, and the undeveloped state of our own jurisprudence meant that general principles had to be relied on. An 1809 Virginia case, *Marks v. Morris,* stated that "It was the common law we adopted, and not English decisions; and we should take the standard of that law, namely, that we should live honestly, should hurt nobody, and should render to everybody his due, for our judicial guide." Indeed, during the War of 1812 some American courts forbade English cases to be cited in court at all.

With a developing jurisprudence, however, the stress toward and need for certainty caused *stare decisis* to be given a higher place in legal thinking. The general conviction of lawyers, also, that they should be able to rely on prior cases, had its effect. Still, the older concept that prior cases must be consonant with good reason supported the idea that a precedent could be overruled by the highest court of a State.

CHAPTER VI

LEGISLATION AND CODIFICATION

Legislation is a new rule or norm of law which takes effect only from the time of passage. It tells us what the law will be from now on. Case law, however, tells us what the law is. Case law, therefore, may be retrospective in effect.

Suppose, for instance, that the legislature passes a law to tax income from source "A". Suppose, in addition, that on the same day a federal court decides that income from source "B", previously thought to be non-taxable, is really taxable. The legislation will affect income from source "A" only in the future. Under the case, however, the tax authorities may validly demand past taxes on income from source "B" from persons who were unaware that they owed the tax, because the federal court had not yet spoken on the matter.

In deciding a case, therefore, a court must take into account the effect its decision will have on existing situations. Sometimes a court will not change a rule it really doesn't like because of the effect it may have, and will suggest that the legislature do so for the future. Sometimes a court will change a rule, but will not apply it retrospectively. Sometimes it will announce that the old rule will apply in the present case, but a new one will apply in the future.

Legislation appears, therefore, to be the most potent way to change law, because it need not conjure with these difficulties. In addition, the legislature has at its beck and call all sorts of assistance that the courts do not have. Legislative hearings, investigative commissions, and professional assistance, give the legislatures many more resources than the courts. In addition, legislatures can respond to problems as they arise, while courts must await litigants who will have the money and fortitude to bring cases before them.

Legislatures, however, are subject to an array of political forces that are not present to the same extent in the case of a court, particularly a court with appointed judges. Legislation that has the potential to raise emotions, ranging from gun control to abortion, has a difficult time whatever is proposed, because strong feelings are aroused on both sides.

ORIGINS OF LEGISLATION

Legislation has a long and honorable tradition. Roman legislation began in the assemblies of the republic, developed through statutes passed by the Senate at the instance of the emperor, and finally became blatantly imperial.

The Anglo–Saxons, from A.D. 600 onward, enacted much that may be viewed as legislation, although a significant portion of it was a recording of pre-existing custom. William the Conqueror and his Council enacted a good deal of legislation, but real impetus came with the reign of Henry II (1154–1189). Legislation was referred to by various names—assizes, constitutions, provisions, and charters. An assize was a meeting, but sometimes the statute that came out of it was also called an assize. Collections of old laws and customs were gathered into constitutions and provisions. A charter, as the name implies, was a grant of rights and privileges, but it may have been merely declaratory of old rights and privileges. Magna Carta, revised four times between 1215 and 1225, was such a document.

The Addition of the House of Commons

The end of the thirteenth century brings us closer to modern legislation. Earlier legislation had taken the form of a grant of rights and privileges by the king and his Council, but under Edward I it became a concurrence of action by the king and the newly emerging Parliament. The word "parliament" means a gathering of persons for the purpose of discussion—holding a parley. Beginning in 1213, representatives of the communes or communities (the shires and boroughs) were called to meet with King John and his Council for the purpose of consenting to measures he desired—particularly when his finances were involved.

Edward I (1272–1307) introduced the procedure of petition and grant. Petitions from representatives of the commons were referred to the chancellor, the judges, the Exchequer, the Justices of Jewry, or other appropriate officers for possible administrative action. Petitions of a more general character were reserved to the king and Council. Relief granted to these general petitions resulted in statutes, a word derived from the Latin *statutum,* meaning "it is decided." At this point in constitutional development, petitions were not drafted in the form of a bill ultimately to be adopted, but in general terms. The form of relief, if any, was determined solely by the king and Council.

The Commons now saw a simple means of increasing its power. It began to refuse to make financial grants until the king had redressed its grievances. Because war was the main cause of financial emergencies, it may be credited with spurring the growth of representative government. By the fifteenth century, the Commons was sufficiently powerful to require that the statute be written out in final form before it granted financial aid; but only after 1500 did the modern period of parliamentary action begin with Commons' drafting its own bills.

The English practice was part of the legal inheritance of the American colonies, and the legacy shows signs of becoming more rather than less important. In the nineteenth century, moreover, a movement began which further enhanced the position of legislation. It was the movement toward codification.

CODIFICATION

Legislation can take many forms. In the dawn of a legislative era, statutes take the form of a reproduction of existing custom. This, for example, was the major content of the Anglo–Saxon dooms and of the Twelve Tables of the Romans. In more developed legal systems, statutes can, as they generally do in this country, take the form of piecemeal legislation designed to solve particular problems in the law. Sometimes these are compiled in one way or another into sets of "codes," but that is not the meaning of the word as it will be used here.

A true code is a new creation that comes about during the maturity of a legal system. When a legal system has developed myriad concepts, principles, and rules, the legal profession sometimes molds them into a unified whole by resolving conflicts, setting forth basic principles, and, in general, consolidating the developments in law to that time.

Early Codes

The first true code was that of Justinian in A.D. 534. It did these very things to Roman law, summarizing legal developments from the time of Cicero (106–43 B.C.) almost to its date. This code came after nearly a millennium of Roman legal history and succeeded an era of mere collections of legislation.

Modern codes probably find their genesis in the Prussian code directed by Frederick the Great (1712–1786). Although not adopted until eight years after his death, it was in effect until 1900. The French were also attracted to codification, and Napoleon's most lasting work was directing the development of the French Civil Code of 1804, which was a model for subsequent codes during the nineteenth century in two dozen countries, as well as the state of Louisiana and the province of Quebec. The later German Civil Code of 1900 was, in turn, the effective model for the modern codes of Japan, Switzerland, Brazil, pre-Communist China, and Greece.

In English law, Jeremy Bentham was the great supporter of codification in the nineteenth century. Save for a few experiments in British India, however, these suggestions came to little except in commercial law.

The idea of codification took hold in the United States in the middle of the nineteenth century. Under the influence of its major proponent, David Dudley Field, codes in separate areas of the law were proposed in numerous states. Instead of one comprehensive code covering all law, the American movement took the form of attacks on five special areas: civil procedure, criminal procedure, civil law, criminal law, and politics. Field's code of civil procedure was the most successful, perhaps be-

cause it was the most needed. It was enacted first
in New York in 1850 and later adopted in about
thirty other states. Civil procedure, encumbered
with the archaisms and anachronisms of English
procedure, needed a total overhaul, not just fragmentary reform. Field's code of criminal procedure met with less success. Only four states adopted all five codes.

Uniform Acts

The form of codification which proved most
adaptable to the Anglo–American legal climate
was even narrower than Field's conception. Rather than to codify all of even the civil law, the route
chosen was to codify particular parts. New York,
for instance, codified its real property law as early
as 1828. Comprehensive penal codes were adopted
by many of the states in the middle of the nineteenth century.

The American Bar Association, formed in 1878,
sought to eliminate differences in law among the
states. Particularly in the area of commercial law
did such differences appear to be ridiculous, but
when it became clear that federal legislation would
be impolitic because a Constitutional amendment
would be necessary, the association turned to the
idea of uniform laws to be adopted by each state
legislature. The thought was that a common statute would lead to uniform law.

A committee was formed to look into the feasibil-
ity of such enactments, and after two years, a

number of states cooperated to form the National Conference of Commissioners on Uniform State Laws. This group proposed a number of such acts including the Negotiable Instruments Act (1896), the Uniform Warehouse Receipts Act (1906), the Uniform Sales Act (1906), the Uniform Stock Transfer Act (1909), the Uniform Partnership Act (1914), and the Uniform Conditional Sales Act (1918). The idea behind the uniform acts was dual: (1) to bring the law into line with current commercial practices and (2) to provide a single law which, if passed by each state in the same form, would lead to uniformity among the various states. These acts and others in the area of commercial law were widely adopted.

But the hopes of the drafters of the uniform acts were defeated in two ways. It is perhaps unfortunate, but also unavoidable, that each state exercised its power to interpret the acts as it saw fit. It was neither unfortunate nor avoidable, however, that commercial practices changed over a period of fifty years, creating the need for new statutes by the 1940's. Instead of proposing new, separate acts, the drafters decided to combine cognate acts into one large statute.

The American Law Institute and the National Conference of Commissioners on Uniform State Laws joined to produce a new Uniform Commercial Code—an integrated statute combining eight previously separate areas. The first draft appeared in 1952 and was adopted by Pennsylvania in 1954.

Further changes were made in 1957 and 1958, and it is now law in all states, and even Louisiana, a civil law state, adopted most of it.

The Anglo–American legal system has resisted the lure of out-and-out codification but has applied the principle of codification to areas in which it is practically and politically feasible. Even in codified areas, however, legal analysis proceeds along traditional Anglo–American lines and does not follow the civil-law approach. The doctrine of precedent rules in the interpretation of these codes, even in the few states that have virtually complete codification. There is also a tendency on the part of lawyers and judges to treat codes as mere declarations of what the law would be in the absence of the code and, sometimes, even to ignore the codes.

In most of our states most of the law is still common law and can be ascertained only by going back to past cases. The extent to which codification will continue to advance is not a matter for safe prognostication, but it appears that the basic modes of legal analysis in the Anglo–American legal system will not change appreciably in the foreseeable future.

INTERPRETATION OF STATUTES

Western legal systems have developed, roughly, three methods of statutory interpretation. On the continent of Europe great stress is given to the opinions of respected jurisprudents on the meaning of their Codes. In England it has been thought

that a statute should be interpreted using strictly
legal knowledge—from the four corners, so to
speak, of the statute. In the United States, try we
to determine the intention of the legislature in
passing the statute.

The early English theory was that the power of
interpretation should lay in the drafter of the
statute. At that time, in England, the royal judges
were part and parcel of the King's Council and
therefore could say that they knew what the statute meant because they were there when it was
drafted. When, however, in the middle of the
thirteenth century the courts assumed a separate
identity, and were no longer intimately associated
with Council, this approach became unworkable as
a practical matter. The courts started to view
statutes as interferences with their province, and
the rule arose that a statute was to be strictly
interpreted. In reality this was an assumption of
power by the courts to check the other depart-
ments of government. The English judges rejected
the idea of looking for the intention of the drafters
and by 1904 we have Lord Halsbury's statement
that "the worst person to construe" a statute "is
the person who is responsible for its drafting."
This assumption of interpretative power was of
great importance in creating the independence of
the judiciary, and vital to our doctrine of the
separation of governmental powers.

In the United States the courts did not adopt
that isolated attitude. Our emphasis on legislative

intention may have been influenced by Constitutional interpretation. Although that document was drafted in secrecy, the effort to have it adopted by the states was accompanied by supporting writings, particularly *The Federalist* by Alexander Hamilton and James Madison, which is still cited in support of interpretive arguments. Because of new conditions not dreamed of when the Constitution was adopted this approach is difficult to apply and has been virtually rejected by some judges and theorists but is vigorously supported by others.

The legislative intention approach, however, can be valuable when applied to relatively recent ordinary statutes. This is particularly true when copies of debates, reports, and the like are regularly published by the legislature involved. The Law Revision Commission of New York State, for instance, issues voluminous reports on proposed legislation, and the National Commissioners on Uniform State Laws has, in the recent Uniform Commercial Code, issued "Comments" on each section which, although not part of the Code itself, may have effect on future judicial interpretation.

The idea of determining legislative intention may well be criticized on the ground that it is really the courts intention that is being determined. This is particularly true when a statute is applied to a case the legislature did not contemplate when drafting the statute—a *casus omissus*. It is also true when the scope of a statute is judicially expanded over time to include factual situations that only vaguely resemble those the legislature had in mind. Judicial restraint, in the face of arguments that would expand its scope and power, is rare.

CHAPTER VII

DOCTRINAL WRITINGS

Although never so important as in the civil law, doctrinal writings hold an important place as a secondary source of law in the Anglo–American legal system. For the very earliest periods, indeed, they are equivalent to true law, for there are no other sources.

Overt legal writing began in England in the reign of Henry I (1100–1135), when several attempts were made to restate the Anglo–Saxon laws in the light of Norman changes. Prime among them, and perhaps the earliest true law book after the Conquest, is a volume known as the *Laws of Henry (Leges Henrici).* Its name is unfortunate, because it derives from the first part of the book which is a reproduction of the Charter of Henry I given at his coronation. The bulk of the book is an attempt to bring the laws of Edward the Confessor up to date.

In the same reign, another book, *Laws of Edward the Confessor,* was compiled by an unknown author. It purported to be a collection of laws in force in England at the time of the Conquest, ascertained by William through jury inquests. Its true nature as a forgery was not discovered until the nineteenth century, after it had influenced writers such as Bracton and Coke, who took what it said as the truth.

FROM GLANVILL TO LITTLETON

If he were in Washington today, Henry II (1154–1189) might be a controversial, vigorous government official. His emotional instability either accounted for, or did not hinder, his great drive, his talent as an administrator and legislator, and his desire to replace the chaos of Stephen's reign with order and to strengthen the central government. During his reign, a *responsalis* could appear for a litigant and direct the procedural aspects of his case, the possessory assizes were created, and legislation stirred with new life.

As a twelfth century administrator, Henry needed records of the emerging common-law system, particularly the most highly developed aspect of it, the Exchequer. When Richard Fitz Neal had been Henry's treasurer for some twenty years, he produced his *Dialogue of the Exchequer,* a basic source of information on early English fiscal matters, but not essentially a law book.

In or about 1187 a treatise appeared which has been attributed to Ranulph de Glanvill, one of Henry's favorites, soon to become his Chief Justiciar. This book was concerned solely with the law as administered in the king's courts. Its importance lay in its manner of organization as much as in the information it gave, for it set the style of legal writing for centuries in the future. At that time there were about fifty royal writs, and this volume was a commentary on them.

The next great book on the common law was the unfinished treatise of 1256 attributed to Bracton. It, too, was a commentary on the writs, which by that time numbered about two hundred and fifty. Bracton's work was much more inclusive than the earlier one, and in some places he appears to have inserted civil-law concepts in order to fill the gaps in the still incomplete English law.

Bracton's work was important at two critical times. When it was written its influence was immense because it was the only authoritative statement of English law in existence. Second, and equally important, was the occasion of its re-publication in 1569, when his emphasis on royal responsibility was a needed counterinfluence to the prerogative powers then being demanded and exercised by the monarch. Lord Coke drew upon Bracton's influence and antiquity in his famous conflicts with the Crown, particularly in invoking his famous statement, "The King is King under God and the law." In the time of Bracton, of course, concepts of divine right in the king were still unknown, and the reaffirmation of Bracton's statement at a time when such claims were being made had a salutary effect.

Two much smaller books, modeled after their predecessors, appeared around 1290–1292. One is called *Fleta* and the second *Britton*. They represent the end of the first era in legal writing and illustrate the beginning of the use of French rather than Latin as the written language of the law. The year 1290 also saw the apocryphal *Mirror of Justices,* which purported to be a description of then current law in the light of the laws of King Alfred. This book, like the *Laws of Edward the Confessor,* is mentioned only because later ages placed much reliance upon it, despite its utter unreliability, until its false nature was revealed by late eighteenth century research.

FROM LITTLETON TO KENT AND STORY

Perhaps in 1481, or only a half-dozen years after the introduction of printing in England, appeared the first edition of Thomas de Littleton's *Tenures.* Its subject, land law, was one with which the author, as a Common Pleas judge, was closely familiar. In passing it may be noted that de Littleton was the maiden name of his mother, not his father. Apparently his father came from a noble but obscure family, but his mother's family was old and famous, and his father upon marriage assumed the more acceptable surname rather than the other way about. The book initiated a new trend in legal writing: organizing a text on a particular subject, not in the form of a commentary on writs but by subject, divided into chapters. After almost a century and a half of use, it was brought up to date and translated from its original law French by Lord Coke in 1628. English legal language is a composite of Latin, French, and English. Latin was the formal language of court documents until 1731; French was the language spoken in the courts until 1362 and did not disappear as the language of legal literature until the sixteenth century. Various editions of *Coke on Littleton* were produced by later editors, adding modern annotations to the prior writings. The work was actively used in the United States until the beginning of the nineteenth century.

Contemporaneously, a new type of comparative law treatise appeared in Sir John Fortescue's *In Praise of the Laws of England,* about 1470. It was a comparative study of English and French law, presumably prepared for the instruction of Prince Edward. Around 1523 this was followed by a philosophical rationale of equity jurisprudence in the *Dialogues between a Doctor of Divinity and a Student of the Common Law* by Christopher St. Germain.

Lord Coke himself wrote the next monumental treatise on English law. The first of his four *Institutes* was the commentary on Littleton, the only one published before his death. His second *Institute* (1642) was a commentary on statutory law; the third (1644) a commentary on criminal law, and the fourth (1644) a history of the courts.

The seventeenth century saw various minor but important legal treatises, some of a practical nature and others concerned with general matters, particularly legal history. Two of the practical

works involved the law merchant and are important because their dates are separated by rapid
progress in the development of the law of negotiable instruments, which is reflected in them. The
first is the *Constitution of the Law Merchant* by
Gerard Malynes (1622); the second is John Marius'
Advice Concerning Bils of Exchange (1651). Historical works include John Selden's *Table Talk* and
Sir Matthew Hale's *History of the Common Law*
and *History of Pleas of the Crown.*

In 1765 appeared the book that was to constitute
a major text for American lawyers until the twentieth century—Blackstone's *Commentaries on the
Laws of England.* These *Commentaries* were discussed in Chapter IV in connection with legal
education.

FROM KENT AND STORY TO THE
PRESENT DAY

The 1820s saw the publication of two important
works in the United States. James Kent published
his *Commentaries on American Law* in four
volumes between 1826 and 1830. He had been a
Justice of the New York Supreme Court and Chancellor of the Court of Equity. Although he followed the four volume format of Blackstone's *Commentaries* his work differed. He traced the
development of American law from English law
and, unlike Blackstone, appreciated continental
civil law. He thought some parts of it were superi-
or to the common law and initiated closer study of

the civil law in the United States. His sixth and final edition was completed in the year of his death, 1845.

Although Joseph Story also called his work commentaries, they were the first legal textbooks. Just as the alphabetically organized discussion of legal procedure, called an abridgment, was followed by an organized discussion of the legal system in the commentary, so the commentary was followed by a reasoned treatment of a particular branch of the law, which is called a textbook.

After Story, authors followed the trend toward specialization foreshadowed centuries earlier by Littleton and given its modern impetus by Story. Today we have, for instance, innumerable treatises such as *Wigmore on Evidence, Williston on Contracts, Prosser on Torts,* and the like. The influence of these men is often so great that they have cast the line of development of the law in many areas. Their contribution is reduction of the mass of the common law, as found in myriad cases, to almost manageable proportions.

One modern and novel experiment in doctrinal writing is the Restatement movement sponsored by the American Law Institute, which was formed in 1923. The Restatement idea was to have a group of learned lawyers, judges, and law professors agree on the essence of the law in particular areas through research and discussion. One scholar was made responsible for the original draft of each topic, on which the others commented until a consensus was obtained. In this way, it was thought, individual personalities and ideas could be submerged in the thinking of the group.

The Restatements do not present new law, in the manner of a statute. Its authors endeavor to present what they consider the best approach from decided cases in all jurisdictions.

A series of Restatements was produced, including those on contracts, agency, torts, and restitution. The effect of each on the law has differed, because some of them are deemed excellent by the profession, and others are not so highly regarded. The Restatements have not altered the traditional approach of the profession to legal analysis; their publication has meant only the addition of another reputable book in each area covered. Courts and lawyers cite the Restatements, but the primary source of law is still the body of cases and statutes.

The law schools of this country produce considerable legal writing in their law reviews. Virtually all law schools publish journals, usually staffed by senior students. Eminent lawyers, judges, and law professors write the lead articles, and students comment on topics and cases of interest. For close analysis, the law reviews are probably more valuable than any other secondary legal source.

*

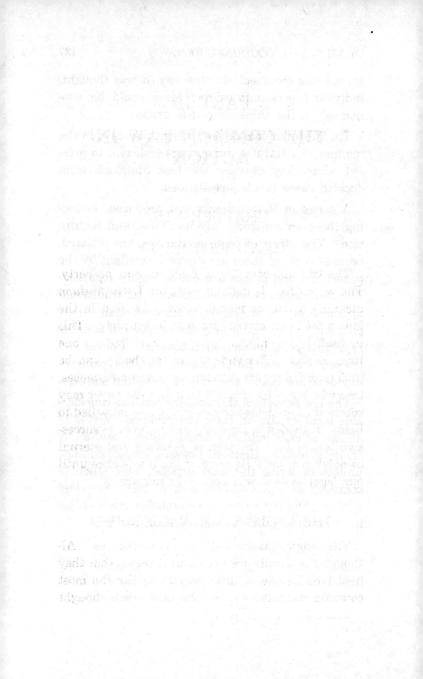

PART III

THE COMMON LAW IN ACTION

CHAPTER VIII

REAL PROPERTY

The concept of a fee is basic in real property. The word "fee" is derived from the Latin *feodum,* meaning a fief, or feudal estate. As used in the law, a fee is an eternal interest in property. This in itself is an enigma, for the fact is that no one lives forever. The eternal-interest theory can be understood only by considering its consequences. One who has a fee can sell land and the buyer may retain it after the seller's death; it can be willed to heirs, or divided in time into any number of successive tenancies. The idea of absolute and eternal ownership of land did not come into existence until our legal system was relatively mature.

THE ANGLO–SAXON BACKGROUND

The Anglo–Saxons did not know the fee. Although the details are not clear, it seems that they held land in one of three ways. By far the most common was folkland. At one time it was thought

129

that this was a system of common ownership, and that inhabitants of the vill annually distributed available tillable land. This was referred to as the mark system. Since the researches of Vinogradoff, a pioneer historian of early English law who wrote at the turn of the century, however, this theory has been abandoned. The truth is more prosaic: folkland means only land held under general or customary law. Since everyone was familiar with it, no one bothered to write down its characteristics, and so its workings are unclear to modern scholars.

It appears conjecturally that the family, rather than the individual, was the unit of ownership. On death of the head of the family, control seems to have passed to the next head of the household. Since there was little trading in land, except in the area held by the Danes, the question of the right to transfer did not arise. There is some indication that when land was given to the Church, the approval of all possible heirs was obtained. That approval, however, may have been merely precautionary and not a legal requisite.

A common form for ownership of land by churches or great men was by formal charter or grant from the king and his witan. This was known as bookland. Bookland was not held in absolute ownership, but it carried rights over the land that continued to be held, at the lowest level, as folkland. To the peasants tilling the soil, a grant of land by book meant merely a change of masters. Since the holders of the book were not interested in doing the actual farming, land held by book was folkland to the actual occupants. Some rights granted by book were to hold court and to collect taxes; the only duties required were the *trinodas necessitas* of (1) rendering military service, (2) repairing bridges within the land, and (3) repairing its roads.

Bookland was governed by the terms of the grant. Sometimes the right to will such land was given, and even when it was not the land could be inherited by heirs. Church land was held by the successors in office of the original grantee. The duration of the bookland estate was controlled by the terms of the book, and if nothing else was said, it was good only for the life of the recipient, after which it reverted to the former owner.

Laen land, the third type, was held for from one to three generations of the superior holder, with the occupier required to turn over to the superior certain quantities of produce. It resembled a modern lease rather than a sharecropping arrangement, except that crops were paid instead of a money rent. It usually was a written arrangement.

This device was widespread because it was one of the few ways to make a profit. Trade was by barter or by professional merchants at the fairs. Interest on the use of money was absolutely forbidden by church and lay law. By acquiring laen land, however, the tenant was entitled to the fruit of the land on payment of the annual dues. For the superior lord (usually a church), the advantage was a steady return from the land for approximately a century. Of course, by the end of three generations, the family holding the tenancy had become so accustomed to it that they considered it family property. It appears that the grantors of laen land occasionally settled the matter with the heirs of the last tenant by a regrant.

THE NORMAN BACKGROUND

The feudal system, as introduced by William the Conqueror, introduced a number of significant changes into this picture. The reasons were a combination of economic, military, and political.

The financial resources of the Anglo–Saxon kings were meagre. They had their own lands, they had lands which they held because of their office as king, they had gifts from their subjects which in course of time assumed a compulsory aspect, they had receipts from their courts as portions of recoveries, and they had their own very high receipts from offences committed against themselves, their property, their family, and their retinue.

William the Conqueror, however, had needs far exceeding those of his predecessors in England. Not only was he king in England, but also Duke of Normandy. This made it necessary to protect not only England, but also large portions of France.

In addition the Normans were definitely superior in governmental administration. While decentralization, a relatively weak though respected king, and power in the nobles was a feature of Anglo–Saxon government, centralization, a strong king, and less power in the nobles was the stress of the Norman kings.

The dominant note of the times was that it was, essentially, a time without money. It was an unmoneyed society. The opposite side of that coin is that it was an agricultural society, and indeed remained so until after Elizabeth I. Agriculture did not lose its dominance until the so-called Industrial Revolution.

The problem was, then, to get things done in the absence of money. The solution was to utilize the basic monopoly—land. William made a claim to own all the land of England, a claim made by no English king before him. Therefore to retain their estates the English nobles had to take an oath of fealty to him. Although this may have been the desire of William, such oaths were not forthcoming. The conquest of England was a slow and tedious process, involving virtual genocide in some parts of England, with the result that twenty years later the number of Englishmen holding land that might be considered manors had been reduced from some five thousand to a total of two.

Instead of land being held by the ruling class merely by virtue of rank, or merely as freemen, land now came to be held in return for services needed by the king. The most important of these were military services, but others could do as well.

Chamberlains, cooks, armorors, arrowmakers, could be given land in return for their services.

Feudalism, therefore, was a two-way relationship. The king granted his lands to this new ruling class, but only in return for certain services. If the services failed, the land returned. What on the surface is a social relationship of lord and man is at its base an economic relationship. The amount of service, or of knights, that was due was in no way based on the value of the land, but was a balance between how much the king needed the vassal and how well the vassal could bargain. It was expected that the vassal would distribute his burden by subinfeudating other vassals who would hold of him. This, however, would not discharge the tenant-in-chief (as those who held immediately of the king were called), for his failure to discharge his obligations would destroy the whole estate, and the vassal and his underlings would all lose their estates as well.

It was from this military-agricultural complex, so to speak, that the political system grew. The king's council was selected from these great men— great because they had been selected by the king, given land by him, and in return promised him services that otherwise he could not buy. In return for his land, the military tenant swore "to become your man for the tenement I hold of you and to bear faith to you of life and members and earthly honor against all other men."

This mode of raising an armed force may have been sufficient for a short expedition; but for permanent defense, a standing army was much preferable. During the twelfth century, actual service of knights was remitted in favor of a money payment called scutage, or *escuage,* and so it remained until the abolition of feudalism in 1660. Scutage was a fixed sum vulnerable to inflation, which appears to be part of the historical process that after a time made it all but worthless. In fact, although not in theory, it appears to have disappeared after 1384, and thereafter armies were raised with funds provided by parliamentary grant. This, as we have seen, was one of the causes of the addition of the House of Commons to Parliament. When feudalism was abolished in 1660, scutage was replaced by a tax on beer. So came a noble institution to a prosaic end.

The theory of knight's service created a real problem on the death of a vassal. Since knight's service was a personal relationship based on the mutual faithfulness of landlord and tenant, must the lord accept the heir of the tenant as the tenant's successor? The son might be an enemy of the lord, or unfaithful, or of doubtful courage. In feudal theory, the lord had a right to choose his vassal. This problem, too, came to be solved by money. On payment of a sum called "relief", the regrant to the heir of the vassal became a matter of right, once the heir had taken an oath of homage or fealty to the lord. Relief also became a fixed sum with diminishing value.

A similar feudal problem was created when the daughter of a vassal married. Suppose she married an enemy of the vassal's lord? This was unthinkable. The marriage must be approved by the lord. But this, too, did not occur without the passing of money, for the hand of the daughter of a landed gentleman was valuable. Marriage to such a woman brought prestige, land, and valuable gifts. Subsequently, and with little warrant even in feudal theory, this right of the marriage fee extended to the marriage of a vassal's son as well.

A further problem arose. Suppose that on the death of the vassal, his son was not of age. The problem could not have been infrequent in those days of short life expectancy. Who should take care of the child? A relative might find it more profitable to kill him than to maintain him, for the relative might inherit the estate. The relative might be an enemy of the lord. The lord, therefore, had the right of wardship; and in return for keeping the ward and educating him in appropriate skills, he had the right to use the child's land until he attained the age of majority without accounting in any way for its profits. This right, like the right of marriage, remained valuable for centuries.

The lord also had the right of aid from his tenant. Financial emergencies were posed by the marriage of his eldest daughter and the knighting of his eldest son (both of which required the giving of gifts and parties) or by his capture and consequent need for ransom money. By the thirteenth century, both the amount of aid and the occasions on which it could be demanded were fixed.

Last, there was the right of escheat. If the tenant was convicted of a felony other than treason, the land, after the profits were taken by the king for a year and a day, escheated to the lord. If the crime was treason, the land was totally forfeited to the king, and the lord lost all his rights even though it was his vassal who had committed the crime.

The tenancies in return for services other than military were known as sergeanties. A tenant in sergeanty, the term "sergeant" meaning "servant", had particular duties to perform. Under early feudalism any lord could create a subordinate sergeanty, but by the fifteenth century sergeanties were held only of the king. Today residual and honorary sergeanties persist in connection with the coronation ceremony. Prestige attended the vassal's position in relation to the prestige of the lord the sergeant served. Relief and aids applied to all sergeanties, and the presence of the rights of wardship and marriage indicated a grand, rather than a petty, sergeanty.

Churches held land in frankalmoign tenure, also called free alms. The church was to perform spiritual services such as the saying of masses for the donor. Obviously, neither relief, wardship, nor marriage could apply to these estates.

Socage tenure was the least of the freehold estates (those protected in the royal courts). It required an oath of faithfulness, but no military service. In fact, no real services may have been due at all, and only a purely formal obligation, such as the giving of one red rose at midsummer to signify the relationship, may have been required. Some sokemen gave a yearly payment, and others gave personal service such as plowing the lord's land. This latter obligation, however, was not on call, as in villein tenure, but due only at specified times.

For a time, each tenant could create a subtenant under him in one of these relationships. A tenant in chief, for instance, holding by military tenure, might give part of his land to another military tenant and part to a church. The prime tenancy, however, remained responsible for the feudal dues and services to the king.

The medieval tenures were, therefore, characterized by a personal relationship between lord (landlord) and man (tenant) which was, theoretically, to last only for the lifetime of the tenant. In fact, however, on payment of relief and the giving of homage, a tenancy could descend to heirs.

Although the estates of villeins were subject to the rules of the manors to which they were bound and were not protected by the royal courts, a word concerning them is in order.

A villein was not a slave. He was free in all respects except against his lord. The criminal law could punish a lord who killed or injured his villein, but the lord could beat or imprison him.

The status of villeinage should be distinguished from an estate in villeinage. Villeinage was an inherited status. It was essentially a relationship between the villein and the lord. The lord was entitled to services at will from the villein, and ordinarily these services were agricultural. The lord could seize the personal property of his villein, but unless that was done the villein was the owner and could deal with his personal property as he saw fit. Lords often permitted their villeins to make wills.

The villein usually held a tract of land on the manor, or at least a cottage. These were, in effect, paid for by the services he rendered the lord. The villein was self-supporting in all other respects. He earned his living from his own lands or, if he was merely a cottager, by working for others than the lord. The lord could, however, eject him from his land. Some villeins were richer than some free persons.

A villein could gain his freedom by manumission. This could be done by charter, or by a grant of land to the villein "and his heirs." Because a villein could not have heirs, a grant to him and his heirs was an admission by the lord that the grantee was a free person. Freedom could be obtained by fleeing the manor and staying in certain towns for a year and a day. He would then be "seised of his freedom."

A freeman could hold land in villeinage and his payment for the land was the same as the villein's—service to the lord at the lord's command, rather than in money or produce. His personal status, however, remained as a freeman. Villeinage was an inherited status, and therefore the child of a freeman who held land in villeinage was also a free person.

INHERITANCE OF LAND

Even though the hurdle of whether land should be heritable or not is overcome by the device of relief, the question remains: who should inherit it? Although the details of Anglo–Saxon law are unknown, one may conjecture from the fact that in all legal systems comparable to ours descendants, not parents or siblings or other kinsmen, are preferred. Also, sons have traditionally been preferred over daughters.

It appears that at the time of the Conquest, parage was the accepted scheme of inheritance. In this form, land descended to all male children of the tenant, subject to the lord's right to approve or disapprove the heirs. The eldest son was responsible for the feudal dues and services on behalf of the group, but his brothers were equal to him. Parage avoided splitting the land among the heirs which, from the feudal point of view, was undesirable: as the process continued, each son might become the holder of a piece of land insufficient to support the feudal dues and services.

Whether an estate in land shall be divided on the death of the tenant has political considerations on both sides. It is easier to deal with one heir than with many; but many weak heirs to partitioned land pose a less potential threat to kingly power than one strong heir to the entire estate. While in France this problem took a long time to resolve, in England it was resolved in favor of impartible primogeniture in the twelfth century, and became firm by the middle of that century during the reign of Henry II. Any scheme other than impartible inheritance was impossible, for how could two persons share one physical service. Primogeniture became the rule in sergeanties also. Where the only heirs were daughters, however, parage continued to be the rule.

From an economic point of view, primogeniture also had an advantage. In an economics of scarcity, is it better that all persons be poor, or that some have wealth? Splitting the land among the sons would be disastrous, for a rich, prolific family might disintegrate into a group of impoverished peasants in the course of a few generations.

Therefore the early institution of primogeniture in England was the sign of a strong and confident monarchy. A weak monarchy might well have preferred that estates be split among numerous persons so that control could more easily be maintained. A strong monarchy was willing to take

that risk. For Henry II the risk did not material-
ize; for King John, early the next century, it did.
But by that time the institution of primogeniture
was too strong to be displaced.

On the other hand the road to primogeniture
may have been predestined by the fact that on the
Continent, kingship was hereditary and descended
to the oldest son. With the Normans, the idea of
hereditary kingship came to England. Its application to military tenures may have been a natural
progression. Then, apparently for economic reasons, primogeniture was applied to villein tenures
(the holdings of peasants on the manors). Socage
was the last tenure to come under primogeniture,
and may have done so purely by example.

Certain areas in England retained old customs.
Kent continued parage under the name of gavel-
kind, and the custom of borough English gave the
land to the youngest son (ultimogeniture).

WHO HAS SEISIN—SERVICE AND DEMESNE

In modern law we know the terms "possession"
and "ownership" fairly well. Both of these terms,
however, are abstract concepts. They do not involve relationships. "Ownership" as such is not a
feudal concept, and possession is not material in
feudal law as far as real property is concerned.

Seisin, however, was a term of relationship. A
lord had seisin of his land, and he could grant
seisin of that land to another. At that point both

lord and tenant had seisin, the incidents of which were controlled by the nature of the relationship between them. The tenant had seisin of the soil itself and the right to take its profits. The lord, on the other hand, was seised, as they said, "in service." His rights arose out of the land—services, scutage, wardship, marriage, or whatever the combination may have been. If these were not forthcoming, the lord had a right to disseise the tenant and take seisin of the soil itself. Therefore no one person "owned" the land, and the term "possession" was not applicable.

Alienation of land

The term "alienation" means, literally, to get rid of something. One may get rid of land by selling it for money, trading it for other land or goods, or by giving it away. It is a voluntary act during life; one cannot alienate land after death.

The scope and power of alienation before primogeniture is not clear. In Anglo–Saxon times it appears that bookland, at least, could be alienated without the consent of the heirs. Norman charters, however, both on the Continent and in England, reveal a propensity toward obtaining the joinder or consent of all heirs—not only sons, but daughters and other relatives who might, perhaps, come into the estate on the death of the owner. Around the year 1200, a swift and mysterious change took place. Glanvill's writings, around 1186, reveal that the old system of approvals still existed, but it had totally disappeared by 1256, the time of Bracton.

The change may have been caused by the introduction of primogeniture and legally facilitated by the doctrine of warranty. Consents, it appears, were needed in order to assure equal division of the inheritance among the sons. Otherwise a father might, by conveyance, prefer one son to another. Primogeniture eliminated this possibility. Furthermore, a father who conveyed land could warrant that he and his heirs would protect the title against attack. The warranty would bind the son, who therefore was unable to regain the land from the purchaser.

It is clear from other evidence that royal judges were highly in favor of free alienation of land, perhaps because of their realization, as the king's men, that free alienation loosened the feudal bonds in the ranks below the king and thus indirectly enhanced the power of the Crown.

Objections to alienation, under feudal theory, could come from the lord, a more potent source. The relationship between lord and tenant was personal; by what authority could the tenant put another person in his place without the lord's consent?

To unravel this problem we must first look at the two possible modes of alienation under feudalism. The first and simplest was a method known as "substitution." Suppose T is the tenant of L. T might, conceivably, sell all his land to X and have

X take his, T's, place as L's tenant. In this way T's seisin of the land would be fully transferred to X and he, T, would be out of the picture. X would now be a vassal of L, directly.

On the other hand T might create a new subtenancy. In such a case he would convey (enfeoff) to X as his own tenant, so that he, T, remained a tenant of L. L would be the lord of T, and T would be the lord of X. This was called "subinfeudation." It created another step in the feudal ladder.

Substitution was inimical to feudal concepts, and subinfeudation could injure the lord's economic position. Substitution was contrary to feudal concepts because if the form of T's ownership was determined by the lord, any changes, theoretically, would have to be made with the lord's consent. In addition, if the lord had granted land to "T and his heirs," he should have been entitled to escheat on the extinction of T's line, and whether T had conveyed the land to anyone else should have been immaterial. More fundamentally, the feudal concept of relationship between lord and man was destroyed by substitution because the lord could not control to whom the land was conveyed by the tenant.

The economic disadvantages to the lord of subinfeudation were of greater practical importance. If a tenant, T, subinfeudated another person, X, for a substantial money payment (which T's lord could not touch) and reserved purely nominal services from X, such as one rose at midsummer, T was still the lord's vassal but the value of the lord's rights plummeted. Scutage was still due and if not paid the land would forfeit to the lord. But the lord's marriage right was reduced to nothing because its value depended on the value of her father's, T's, estate, which was now nominal. If T died, relief to be paid by the heir was based on the value of T's estate, and if the heir was a minor the lord's wardship duties continued but his right to profits was reduced to the right to receive one rose per year. If T committed a felony, the escheated estate that went to the lord was valueless. Or T may have subinfeudated a church in return for its promise to say prayers for the repose of his soul. This did not benefit the lord, and the church did not marry, die, or commit felonies.

A still more involved evasive practice took place. A tenant might convey land to a church with the understanding that the church would subinfeudate him for lesser services. The result was that the superior lord now had the church for a tenant, with the resulting loss of feudal dues, but the erstwhile tenant still had the benefit of the land with his obligations considerably reduced. The church now stood as an intermediate tenant between the superior lord and the tenant.

Protests were made against all these practices. The 1217 edition of Magna Carta spoke out against them, the Petition of Barons presented to the king at Oxford in 1258 requested a remedy for unauthorized gifts by their tenants to clerics, and the

Provisions of Westminster in 1259 purported to give them a remedy, but was ineffectual.

On the Continent, the lord's consent to alienation appears to have been the established practice, but perhaps in a newly conquered country where the lands of all enemy English lords were forfeited, it was expected that subinfeudation would be used as the primary means of filling the feudal ranks. So long as subinfeudation (for this was the normal mode of alienation) was not abused, objections were not effective.

Only in 1279, with the Statute of Mortmain, was the practice of giving lands to churches even impeded. Thenceforth, gifts to churches were to be made only by express license from the king, obtained on payment of a fee. These licenses, however, were freely granted.

During the thirteenth century, it became increasingly clear that tenants in chief of the king could not alienate their lands without royal consent. While lesser lords who were prejudiced in their rights could, in turn, alienate to the injury of their own lords, only the king was no man's tenant. Therefore the ultimate effect of the practice would have fallen on him. This he would not permit.

The 1290 statute *Quia Emptores Terrarum* (because purchasers of land) finally stopped the practice of subinfeudation among even lesser lords. It forbade subinfeudations of fee simple estates. A tenant in fee could still subinfeudate, however, by granting an estate less than a fee, such as a life estate or an estate in tail. The statute permitted free alienation of part of the estate by substitution if the services due the superior lord were apportioned according to the quantities of land remaining in the parties' hands. The statute did not apply to lands held directly of the king, and therefore tenants in chief could not alienate in any manner without the king's consent.

The statute implicitly recognized that feudalism had ceased to be a military-social system. Actual military service had been changed to money payments, and land was considered to be a source of income. Under feudal theory, the seller of land was in reality the purchaser of services for which he paid in land; now the purchaser was buying land, for which he paid in services. The statute recognized this by proscribing subinfeudation in fee estates, the feudally less harmful but economically more harmful mode of alienation, and permitting alienation, which was not in line with feudal theory, but quite in line with economic reality.

Abolition of subinfeudation could have been popular only with the king and the tenants in chief, for the king had no dues to avoid, and the tenants in chief, by that date, could not avoid them. Yet the statute was a good compromise. The lord's economic rights could not be diminished, and yet the tenant could alienate land.

The statute may have been beneficial in a more subtle way. The abolition of subinfeudation in fee simple estates tended to limit the number of rungs in the feudal ladder reaching down from the king to the actual tenant in demesne. This was a political benefit in that it kept down the number of lords and barons, so that those who remained were closer to the royal government. Natural processes of extinction of lines and escheat of estates to the immediately superior lords assisted this process.

THE USES OF A FEE

The rights of the heir to inherit land and of the owner to sell it are two essential elements of the fee interest. If land were not inheritable, the most one could convey would be an estate for the duration of one's own life, for that is all one would own. If land were inheritable but could not be sold, its value would be considerably reduced, for value consists, at least in part, of what one can expect a sale to bring.

A fee owned by one person is called a fee simple. When owned with another person it may be a tenancy in common, a joint tenancy, a coparceny, or a tenancy by the entireties, depending on the relationship between the owners and the incidents of ownership.

A tenancy in common is ownership by more than one individual in which shares need not be equal, and in which each owner has full control to sell, encumber, or will his individual portion. A joint tenancy is a second form of multiple ownership in which the shares must be equal and derived from the same conveyance, and in which each party may sell his own portion (thus converting it into a tenancy in common between the new party and the old), or he may encumber it, but he cannot will it. On death, the decedent's portion is divided equally among the remaining owners. Coparceny, long obsolete, is the equal interest inherited by daughters when, under the scheme of primogeniture, there was no male heir.

A tenancy by the entireties is ownership of land by husband and wife, and neither can sell, encumber, or will his interest. At the death of one, the land belongs to the survivor in fee simple.

The Life Estate

Since a fee is eternal ownership, an owner of a fee can divide it temporally into successive interests. He may, for instance, convey the land to another for the duration of that other person's life. It should be noticed that a life estate may, in actuality, be shorter than a lease for years, such as one for fifty years. But in contemplation of law any estate for life is more important than any for a term of years. A term of years is not a freehold.

There is a variation of the life estate known as the estate *pur autre vie,* or estate for the life of another. Suppose, for instance, that A has an estate for his life and grants it to B. On the valid principle that A cannot grant more than he has, B gets what A had, which is an estate for the duration of A's life.

By definition, a life estate always has a fee above it. It is implied that on the death of the life tenant, the land will revert to the original grantor, who is the owner of the fee, or to his heirs. Also, any number of life estates can be carved out of a fee. For instance: A, an owner in fee, may provide B with a life estate which is to go to C on B's death, to D on C's death, and so on.

The life estate was so common in the early days of our law that it was presumed to be granted merely by the statement that the land was conveyed "to A." A fee could be created only by the words "to A and his heirs." The magic words "and his heirs" remained essential until very recent times in order to create a fee in the common-law jurisdictions of the United States.

Reversions and Remainders

In any type of conveyance, if the owner does not dispose of the complete fee, he necessarily retains a reversion. If he gives a tenancy for one year, the rest of the infinity of time is his in reversion. If he gives a life estate, the fee reverts to him or his heirs at the death of the life tenant. Seisin, which referred to possession as applied to land, and the duty to perform the feudal dues and services were in the reversioner. A reversionary interest must be distinguished, however, from escheat. Escheat gave the land to the superior lord on the death of a tenant in fee who died without any heirs, either lineal or collateral.

A remainder is the equivalent concept when the infinity of time left after the granting of a lesser estate is in the hands of someone other than the donor. If A gives a life estate to B, with a remainder to C and his heirs, A rids himself of all his interest in that land. There is nothing left to revert to him. B has a life estate which, as the first estate to come into enjoyment, is called the particular estate. C has the remainder—all that is left over after B's life estate determines (ends). It is a vested remainder because it is not subject to any condition other than the death of B (which is sure to happen); and if C is also dead at the time of B's death, his heirs take the fee in his stead. If he has no heirs, the estate escheats. Seisin and the duty to perform feudal obligations were in the remainderman.

A contingent remainder, on the other hand (1) goes to a person or persons whose identity is uncertain at the time of the grant, or (2) is to come into being after the happening of an uncertain event in the future.

An example of the first type is a grant to A for life, with a remainder to the heirs of B. Since no one can have an heir until death, the recipients of that estate in remainder are not known, and a contingent remainder is created. By the middle of the fifteenth century, the common law had worked out a solution to this type of contingency. If the condition was actually met by the time of the determination (ending) of the particular (first) estate, it was valid. If B was dead by the time of A's death, the defect was cured, and the heirs of B (who were then known) took a fee. If he was not dead, the land reverted to the original grantor.

An example of the second type is a grant to A for life and, in case B survives him, to B and his heirs. Here the recipient of the remainder is certainly B, but B will not take this estate unless he survives A, and this is an uncertain future event.

But who had seisin? Generally, in contingent remainders, seisin was held to be in the life tenant until his death. This, of course, meant that the estate might be destroyed by escheat or forfeiture if the holder of the life estate committed treason or felony or if he conveyed the land before the contingency occurred.

Whether the contingency could be something other than the death of the holder of the life estate was long a puzzle to the common law. Various rules concerning "repugnant" conditions arose when these matters came before the courts in the sixteenth century and thereafter, all subject to numerous refinements and uncertainties. Such remainders were finally protected by creating trusts to hold them until the occurrence of the contingency.

The modern rules on remainders protect both vested and contingent remainders of all legal types, and the basic problem is to make certain that the time in which they will ultimately vest, or become certain, is not outside the legal limit. For

this an admirably involved rule known as the Rule
Against Perpetuities was developed out of the *Duke
of Norfolk's* case (1682). Basically, its object is that
all estates are to vest at a date not later than
twenty-one years after the end of a life (or the last
of several lives) in being at the time of the creation
of the estate.

The Estate in Fee Tail

Following a long period of development, the details of which are not absolutely clear, the provisions of the Statute of Westminster II known as *De
Donis Conditionalibus* (1285) permitted the creation of the estate in fee tail. The origin of the
device apparently lay in the desire of parents to
assist a young couple in the founding and perpetu-
ation of a family, but it became a method of perpet-
uating a family's feudal status.

The estate in tail, or entail, restricted ownership
of land to a particular family line. If the line ever
(in theory at least) became extinct, the land was to
revert to the original grantor's line. His interest
was called a "possibility of reverter" rather than a
reversion because in a reversion seisin was in the
reversioner, but in an estate tail seisin was in the
tenant in tail. The form of the grant was, for
instance, "to A and the heirs of his body." This
was called a tenancy in tail general. As Lord Coke
translated from Littleton:

Tenant in taile generall is, where lands or tenements are given to a man, and to his heires of his

bodie begotton. In this case it is said generall taile, because whatsoever woman, that such tenant taketh to wife, (if he hath many wives, and by every of them hath issue) yet everie one of these issues by possibilitie may inherit the tenements by force of the gift; because that everie such issue of his bodie ingendred.

An estate in tail could also be given to a woman and the heirs of her body by whatever husband.

On the other hand, "Tenant in taile speciall is, where lands or tenements are given to a man and to his wife, and to the heires of their two bodies begotton. In this case none shall inherit by force of this gift, but those that be engendred between them two." If the grantee was a daughter or female cousin of the grantor, a statement that the conveyance was in "frankmarriage" was sufficient to accomplish the same object.

Other variations were possible: an estate tail male, restricted to males in the line (if these lapsed, the estate reverted to the donor's line); an estate tail female, restricting it to the female line; and estate tail special male, in which the estate went only to the male heirs of a given married couple, and so forth.

The theory of the fee tail gave rise to some interesting questions, and to some even more interesting consequences. Suppose land is granted to "X and the heirs of his body." What are X's rights? Suppose X purports to sell the land, what will the purchaser receive?

Before 1285 it appears that X, in such a case, had a life estate which rose to a fee if and when a child was born to X. After the birth of a child, therefore, X could convey a full fee. It may be that the 1285 statute was intended to restrict X from being able to convey a fee, but to have the estate turn into a fee when X died and his child inherited. This, however, runs up against legal logic. Either the child takes through his father, X, or takes after him as in the manner of a successive purchaser. If he takes through his father, the feudal incidents, particularly relief, are owing. If he takes after his father, as a purchaser, feudal incidents are not owing. There would in that latter case have been two successive conveyances in the same transaction—one to the father for life, and a second to the child in fee to take effect at the father's death. But a decision not long after 1285 indicated that not only the father, but also his child could not alienate a fee. The result of this was to preserve the feudal dues owed to the lord, and the price was to make the land inalienable in fee. At first the restriction on alienation was to the third generation, but by the end of the fifteenth century an estate tail continued until extinction of the blood line.

Some remarkable effects flow from this conclusion. We start with the proposition that we only own what we can sell. A corollary of that proposition is that our creditors can only attach for our debts that which we own. In the estate tail, as developed, the person having seisin of the land could not sell it in fee—only an estate *pur autre vie* (for his own life). Therefore if the person having seisin committed treason, the estate tail could not be forfeited to the king because the treasonous person did not own it. He only had a life estate. In the same manner if the person having seisin got into debt his creditors could not attach the land, and if he went bankrupt the land was not among his assets. If he committed a felony, the land did not escheat to the lord.

The estate tail, therefore, was protection against moral, political, and economic catastrophe. Exemption from bankruptcy was abolished in 1654, from forfeiture for treason in 1534, but the estates were still protected from escheat due to felonies to the time of Blackstone.

By the early sixteenth century the device of the common recovery had developed. This made it possible for the tenant in fee tail, in many cases, to convey a fee simple estate to a third party. The common recovery was a completely fictitious suit— a pious fraud. The device went through many stages, but the simplest example is the single voucher. Suppose, for instance, that A was in possession as a tenant in fee tail and desired to convey a fee to B. B would sue him for the land, alleging that A had no legal title to it and that it really was owned by B. A would enter an appearance and call upon X (from whom, he alleged quite fictitiously, he had purchased the land) to defend

the title in accordance with the warranty given by
X to A. This process was called vouching to warrant. X was called the common vouchee, because
he usually was the court crier and frequently acted
in this capacity. X would appear but would subsequently default, whereupon judgment would be giv-
en to the plaintiff, B, against A, and the court
would give another judgment to A against X, presumably for lands of equal value, because of X's
breach of warranty in defaulting. X, of course,
was in fact not expected to give A anything. The
suit resulted in the conveyance of a fee estate to B.
This device could also be used, in a more complicated form, to extinguish or bar the entail without a
sale. In either form, the process was called "barring the entail."

The combination of the rule that an estate in fee
tail could not be sold, encumbered, or escheated to
the detriment of the heirs, coupled with the practical fact that it could be converted into a fee by the
device of the common recovery, made it a most
valuable form of ownership. It could be a bulwark
against disaster, a relatively untouchable asset,
and at the same time perfectly marketable.

There were, however, families who desired that
land remain within the family from generation to
generation. Indeed, until modern times much
English land was held in this fashion. To do so,
however, required an appeal to the profit motiva-
tion of heirs who might otherwise get money by
selling their patrimonies. This could be done by a

father conveying the land to himself for life with a monetary charge on the land in favor of his son, the land then to go to the son for life, and then to future sons via an estate tail male. On the death of the father, the son and grandson can collude in a common recovery and repeat the process with the son getting a life interest, a monetary charge in favor of the grandson to induce him to join in the procedure, the land then to go to the grandson for life, and an estate tail male for the future. In this way each generation could guarantee that the estate would be kept in the family until at least twenty-one years after the birth of a great-grandson.

The estate tail was not looked upon with favor in the United States. Most states merely provided that a conveyance to "X and the heirs of his body" gave rise to a fee simple. Other states interpreted such a conveyance as a life estate in the grantee followed by a remainder in fee simple in his issue. In fewer states the fee tail will have its common law effect if left alone, but the tenant in tail may convey a full fee by a regular conveyance—thus barring the entail without the necessity for a fictitious common recovery. If he dies, however, before selling the land it will go to his issue. In still fewer states the estate tail is deemed to create a life estate in the tenant, which becomes a full fee once a child is born.

Conclusion

These illustrations of the life estate, estate in tail, and vested and contingent remainders are merely a few examples of the uses to which the concept of the fee, the eternal interest in land, might be put. Others include such esoteric matters as estates subject to conditions subsequent, conditions precedent, implied (unexpressed) reversions, rights of entry, and possibilities of reverter. These devices are by no means antiquities, but today they are basically the subject matter of that branch of equity known as the law of trusts, for future interests in purely legal estates are rare indeed.

DOWER AND CURTESY

In a society in which the family is the basic unit, and in which income derives from private property, some provision must be made for a surviving spouse. Primogeniture, by the twelfth century, had become the dominant mode of devolution of real property at the death of the owner, and real property was the dominant source of private income. Had no provision been made for the surviving spouse, therefore, he or she would have been penniless.

Today the problem is not nearly as acute. Although many families obtain income from their own businesses and investments, most are employed by others and have relatively little property—their homes, personal property in consumer

goods, and some investments. Insurance and Social Security are very important forms of protection against the financial problems created by the
death of the wage earner. Today the surviving
spouse has rights in "family" property of one of
two types. Many states follow an essentially civil
law concept of community property. In such states
each spouse is entitled by right to one-half of the
earned (onerous) property of the other, although
not to property obtained by such means as inheritance (lucrative property). In common law states
the surviving spouse who has not deserted the
other is entitled by statute to a certain minimum
of all the property of the deceased spouse. A will
that attempts to disinherit the surviving spouse, or
to give her or him less than the statutory minimum, is ineffective. He or she is entitled to this
minimum share. In addition, of course, husband
and wife may own property as tenants by the
entireties and that property automatically goes to
the survivor.

At common law the widow's right in her husband's property was known as "dower", and the
widower's right in his wife's property as "curtesy."
According to Pollock and Maitland, the idea may
have grown out of an earlier gift from husband to
wife at the time of the marriage, perhaps after
negotiating with the wife's parents. It appears
that the gift was not valid unless given "at the
church door"; perhaps a way to insure sacramen-
tal marriages. A remnant of this exists in the

traditional marriage ceremony that includes the pious promise of the bridegroom that "with all my worldly goods I thee endow." By the middle of the thirteenth century this had become the widow's right to a one-third interest for life in all the lands owned by the husband at any time during the marriage.

This rule applied only to real property, and not to personal property. This is because during the twelfth century jurisdiction over personal property at death passed to the church courts. Even when, in the sixteenth century, the lay jurisdiction of the church courts was taken over by the national courts, differences in the law of decedents' estates continued between real and personal property down into the twentieth century. Only with quite modern statutes giving the surviving spouse minimum rights in all property of the deceased spouse, personal and real, did this anachronistic distinction cease.

The concomitant right of the husband in his wife's real property was called curtesy. This right was more extensive than the widow's right. Instead of a one-third interest in land for life, the husband was entitled to all the wife's lands for the duration of the marriage, and this extended to his life as well when she died if a child had been born of the marriage even though the child predeceased the parents.

The source of this right of curtesy may have come from the general idea that the husband was the guardian of the wife and of his children. This idea also has its liturgical remnant in the traditional Christian marriage ceremony which asks "Who gives this woman?"—symbolic of the transfer of guardianship of the woman from her father or close male relative to the bridegroom.

To guarantee these rights the land of either was inalienable without the consent of both. A husband could not sell land owned by him alone unless his wife gave her consent. The consent was given privately before a judge, in order to assure as much as possible that it was given of her own free will. The husband could, however, give an estate which could last for his own life in land which was, or had become, his wife's, if a child had been born of the marriage, but he could not sell a full fee in such land unless his wife gave her consent before a judge. The wife, however, could not during her husband's life, convey her expectant dower interest. Neither dower nor curtesy applied to equitable estates, trusts, partnership real estate or joint estates.

THE LEASEHOLD ESTATE

Suppose a tenant, called the lessee, is ejected from the premises by the landlord, called the lessor, during the term of the lease? Or suppose the lessor sells the land to another person who ejects the tenant? Or suppose a third party claims that the land is really his and ejects the tenant? What rights has the tenant in each case?

Today the answer to these questions is clear. The tenant has a definite interest in the land during the term of the lease. It is his in accordance with the terms of the lease. The landlord may not eject him, and the landlord's sale to another is subject to the lease unless a clause in the lease specifically permits such a sale. A third person who claims the land must sue the landlord and if the claimant proves superior title to the landlord's the land will belong to the claimant. These answers, however, were not devised in modern form until the nineteenth century, although the general line of tenant's rights were becoming clear in the seventeenth century.

In the twelfth century, on the contrary, the tenant could get the land back only if the landlord ejected him. That would have been a breach of covenant—the "contract" by which he had the land. If the landlord sold the land to another person the tenant could not get the land back, only damages for breach of covenant. The tenant had no right against the third person. Such rights were in the landlord only. If, presumably, the landlord got the land back from the third party, he would have to return it to the tenant in accordance with the terms of the covenant.

Compare the tenant's position with that of the holder of an estate for life. The life tenant had an estate in the land itself. It was his for the duration of his life. If his grantor (not landlord) ejected him, he could sue for its return, and if the grantor sold the land to another it did not affect the life estate of the life tenant. If another person claimed the land was his, he had legal means to contest that contention.

The reason for this difference, although speculations are available, is not clear. Terms of years could involve large sums of money, sometimes involved fealty although not homage, were often between important individuals, and the lessee had a type of seisin of the land. But he was given no protection against his disseisin by another. The possessory assizes did not apply. He was not seised of a freehold, which were the only estates protected by the possessory assizes.

Various reasons have been given. Maitland thought that perhaps this was because early English judges, in viewing the term of years, modelled it after the Roman usufruct—a right to receive the benefits of something without actually owning it. A somewhat more attractive notion is that of Jouon des Longrais, who ascribed economic reasons. According to Longrais, the term of years was a base and unlovely device which enabled lenders, at a time when interest on loans was prohibited by lay and canon law, effectively to evade the laws against usury. This could be done, according to him, by taking in return for a loan of money a lease of an impecunious landowner's land from which the tenant could realize a profit which, had the transaction been in the form of a loan, would have been usurious. The protection of the posses-

sory assizes, in this view, was restricted to estates
that provided the basis for the economic support of
the family. Leases for this purpose did not become
significant until the end of the fourteenth century.

It seems clear, however, as Milsom has pointed
out, that the lease developed from a pure covenant
or contract to a property right. The early lease
was a contract, pure and simple, between the landlord and the tenant. On the death of the landlord
his lord's rights to the land were not affected.
Remedies under covenant were restricted to enforcing the covenant made by the landlord. If the
tenant had been ejected by the landlord recovery of
the land was possible; but if the landlord had
conveyed the land to a third party recovery of the
land was impossible and the only remedy was
damages. Because the third party had no covenant with the tenant, no remedy was available
against him.

This changed in 1235 with a new writ called
quaere ejecit infra terminum that gave the tenant a
remedy against a grantee from the landlord. Not
much later the writ *de ejectione firmae* was devised, giving the tenant an action against all third
persons but providing only for damages, not the
return of the land. *Quaere ejecit,* therefore, appears to have given a limited property right in the
land to the tenant, but *de ejectione firmae* merely
recognized a wrong to him.

Milsom, in his *Historical Foundations of the
Common Law,* points out a very real and practical

problem. If the tenant had an action against the third party, he would effectively be defending the title of his landlord and loss of the suit would mean the landlord's loss of the land.

It was not until the very close of the fifteenth century that the courts enlarged the scope of *de ejectione firmae* to include recovery of the land itself. A "contractual" right had developed into a remedy for a wrong which in turn had become in essence a proprietary action.

The Writ of Ejectment

This development in turn spelled the beginning of the end for the old possessory actions—novel disseisin and its offspring, and the various writs of entry. Litigants who wanted to bring disputes over land titles to court, developed the writ of ejectment during the sixteenth century which, although it appears to be a fabric of involved legal contortions, doubtless was more satisfactory to all concerned than the older methods, and was used into the nineteenth century.

The writ of ejectment involved a series of fictions. A fiction is an allegation that everyone knows is untrue but that must be accepted by all the parties. As it was finally worked out, the person claiming the land, A, would allege that he had made a lease of the land to X. X did not in fact exist. X in turn would allege that he had been ejected from the land by Y. Y did not exist. Y then claimed he was a lessee of B, who was the real defendant. B, the defendant, as a condition to permission to defend against the claimant's suit, had to confess the lease, entry and ejection (ouster). Consequently there were no actual leases, tenants, or ousters. The title of the suits was merely John Doe (fictitious name) on the demise (lease) of Smith v. Brown. Modern reforms in the nineteenth century made these fictitious allegations unnecessary, and provided for direct suit by the claimant against the alleged owner.

WILLS OF LAND

Two sticks of the bundle called ownership—alienation and inheritance—having been examined, consider now a third: the right to devise land by a will.

We must first distinguish between succession and testamentary distribution. Succession is a scheme, customary or legislative, for the devolution of a deceased person's property. It prescribes one's heirs. A testament, or will, is a voluntary provision for the disposition of one's property at death. A modern will is, by definition, revocable until death. In succession the law designates one's heirs, but a testator names his own heirs. A person who dies without a will is said to die "intestate."

It appears that the concept of a will as an instrument by which one can voluntarily make one's own heirs does not develop until a given civilization becomes at least partly commercial. Babylonian law, for instance, did not know wills. Even a sale of property was not binding on the heirs who could regain it on repayment of the purchase price. Solon's laws for Athens restricted inheritance to the family, and one could not disinherit a son or divide property at death other than equally between sons.

Roman Law

In early Roman law, all legal rights over property were vested in the family, not in individuals; but they were exercised by the father, who was also responsible for family worship. There were no testaments, and succession was controlled by custom. On the death of the father, not only control of family property but also the personality and position of the father devolved upon his successors. The first in line of succession were those who were in his legal power during his lifetime. On his death they became *sui juris,* or independent. If there were no successors, adopted or natural, succession passed to the *agnati,* or those descended from a common male ancestor. In the absence of *agnati* it went to the *gens,* or clan, which was a group claiming a common remote ancestor, either actual or mythical.

The fear that all these might fail and that there would be no one to tend one's grave, to the great torment of his spirit, brought about the device of adoption, which, being irrevocable, resembled a will only in that it was a voluntary act. The next step was provision for a public declaration of the person to become the heir. This was followed, in turn, by an adaption of the early Roman sale of property: the *patrimonium* (all the powers of the father over property, family, and worship) was transferred in the presence of a public official to a third person who was to distribute it after the father's death in accordance with the father's express wishes. Subsequently, under the praetors, a written document, or testament, was permitted.

This process accompanied the general individualization of property. The transition from family ownership to individual control and ownership took place as Roman society gradually changed from a small, closely knit group to an enormous trading and commercial society in which family ownership had to cease.

Anglo–Saxon Succession and "Wills"

Throughout this and the following discussion, wills of land and wills of personal property will be treated separately. They were subject to different rules and policies. Remnants of this division continued into the twentieth century.

Little is known about succession and wills (called a *cwide*) in Anglo–Saxon times. Succession to personal property was by customary rules that have not come down to us. Even in 1215, chapter 27 of the Magna Carta tersely states that "If any free-man shall die intestate his goods shall be distributed by his nearest of kindred and his friends, and by the view of the Church." That surely gives us no clue how the goods were to be distributed.

There were Anglo–Saxon wills of personal property, but their form is not known. It is not even known whether they were effective, as they often called upon the king or a lord to see that they were carried out.

Anglo–Saxon land could be held as folkland, a holding that was controlled by custom. Such land could not be sold without royal consent, nor could it be willed. Bookland was given to one by the king and the witan by a written charter, or book. The incidents of bookland varied, but in general bookland could be sold or left by will. The third variety of land-holding was laen-land, given to a person for from one to three lives. By its terms it could not be willed.

Another mode of transferring land at death was the *post obit* (after death) gift. A person in good health could make a present gift, not revocable, that would take effect only at the person's death. Normally a written document, it had neither a settled form nor a settled theory. The donee was often a church.

Norman Wills

By the beginning of the thirteenth century, a rule against the willing of land was coming into being. Glanvill, in 1187, spoke out against death-bed dispositions of land on the ground that at such a time, when a person is perhaps in pain and definitely in dire peril, his judgment may be impaired to the detriment of his natural heirs. The reason probably was the desire of the royal courts to protect the natural heirs.

At a later date, another reason was ascribed for the prohibition against wills of land. The doctrine of seisin, as developed, required an actual physical transfer of possession of land, or of some token thereof, such as a twig or piece of turf, at a formal ceremony on the land or in sight of it, to make an effective transfer. This ceremony, known as livery of seisin, is impossible, of course, in a will of any type.

Despite this rule borough land could be willed. Some boroughs even had registers of wills in which wills of land were recorded. Glanvill's reason for the royal rule would seem to apply equally to the boroughs, for it is scarcely likely that clergy in the boroughs would be less avaricious than those in the country. It may be that this distinction was affected by the fact that in the boroughs land was an article of commerce as freely bought and sold as were chattels. It was purely an economic asset. In the country, however, land under the jurisdiction of the royal courts was in addition the determiner of one's place in government and in society. It was the desire of the royal courts to enforce primogeniture, so that not only the wealth but the position of the ancestor devolved upon the heir. Indeed, in the thirteenth century the notion was expressed that even in the boroughs only purchased land could be willed, and that inherited land could not be willed.

What is clear is that the borough courts excluded the church courts from jurisdiction over wills concerning burgage tenements. It is also clear that royal policy gave wide discretion to the boroughs to create their own law in this as well as in other matters.

Disposition of chattels effective at death, however, continued throughout England. Because of the connection of such gifts with deathbed distributions, the last rites of the Church, and gifts to the Church, the Church came to have jurisdiction over them. It developed the law concerning wills of personal property and executorships until the abolition of its jurisdiction over such matters after the Reformation, when control passed into the hands of Chancery.

USES AND WILLS

The concept of the use is simple. It merely required that the owner convey property to another person or persons with the understanding that the owner (donor) or someone he designated shall have the use of or profit from the property, while for all other purposes the recipient shall be considered the owner. The recipient held the property to the use of the beneficial owner or, as we would say today, in trust for the beneficiary. The beneficiary might be the donor himself. In technical terms the donor was called the feoffor to uses, the recipi-

ent the feofee to uses, and the beneficial owner the
cestui que use. Today they are called, respectively,
the settlor, trustee, and beneficiary.

The roots of this device, to which analogies can
be found in Roman law, lie earlier than our court
records. There is reason to believe that it was
used by the Crusaders, who conveyed lands to
friends for their own convenience during their absence. Although one could not will land, he could
instruct his friends concerning its disposition if he
did not return from his holy venture. The common-law courts, to be sure, did not enforce this
intention and recognized only the transfer of the
legal title. At the earliest period, uses may have
been enforced by the ecclesiastical courts, but by
the reign of Henry III (1216–1272) the Courts
Christian no longer had any jurisdiction over this
arena of litigation. After that reign, enforcement
lay only in the conscience of the friends or by the
persuasion or authority of their confessors, because
this obligation was recognized by the Church and
was the subject of spiritual sanctions. In the middle of the fifteenth century, however, uses began to
be enforced in Chancery, and subsequent development of this area of law took place in that forum.

The device could be utilized to accomplish a
variety of purposes. As mentioned, one could effectively direct the transfer of land at death by
providing that the feofee to uses hold the land
until the feoffor's death and then convey it to the
cestui que use, and thereby circumvent the rule

against wills of land. The beneficial owner could be directed to pay the donor's debts after death, thus making it easier for the donor to borrow money. It could be used until 1377 to hide property from creditors. Until 1391 uses could be created in favor of churches without royal license, and until 1393 were not forfeitable for the treason of the cestui que use. Until 1489 it could be used to avoid reliefs and wardship which would have been due had the feoffor to uses remained the owner. Because of the secrecy of the device, however, attempts to forestall the less benign uses of the device were ineffective.

THE STATUTE OF USES AND THE STATUTE OF ENROLLMENTS

In 1536, after a long period of royal dissatisfaction with the device of the use because of its employment to avoid wardship and marriage dues, a statute was enacted that, it was hoped, would abolish it. The Statute of Uses provided that if A conveyed land to B to the use of C, the use in the hands of B was immediately executed and full title to the land went to C. The device was, therefore, not usable as a substitute for a will. If A conveyed land to B, with instructions to reconvey it to C at A's death, it acted as an immediate conveyance to C. This was, of course, not at all what A wanted.

Also, in 1536, the Statute of Enrollments was enacted which provided the basis for the modern mode of conveying land. It had for some time been clear that if A agreed to sell land to B, with payment of the price and actual transfer of the land to take place at a later date, B immediately obtained the equitable title (because uses were enforced only in the equity [Chancery] court) and A became the holder of the bare legal title. Therefore the provisions of the Statute of Uses would mean that once A's purpose for holding legal title had been fulfilled, the Statute of Uses would execute the use and convey full title to B. The purpose of A in holding the bare legal title was as security for the purchase price. Once the price was paid, title, by virtue of the Statute of Uses, would immediately "shoot" into the buyer. This would have meant that secret conveyances of land could be accomplished, which the Statute was designed to stop because it was contrary to royal policy. The classic mode of conveying land had been livery of seisin, which required a type of ceremony on the land by which the vendor handed over a clod of earth or a twig to the vendee, with appropriate words of enfeoffment (transfer) presumably in view of the public. Other means involved court proceedings which were also on record. The bargain and sale, however, as this device was called, could have avoided publicity. Consequently the Statute of Enrollments provided that such conveyances were ineffective unless recorded. If not recorded the first owner, A, would still have full title and could effectively convey legal title to a third person thus defrauding B. This started the era of the written conveyance, recorded in a public office, and effectively spelled the end of the older modes of conveying titles to land.

It should be noted that the Statute of Uses still has an effect in this area. If A agrees to sell certain land and buildings to B, with final transfer (called a closing, or settlement) to take place at a later date, what are the rights of the parties if the buildings are destroyed by fire in the interim? Modern law states that although the vendor is the holder of the bare legal title, he is merely holder as trustee for the buyer who is the beneficial owner. Therefore the buyer must pay the full price for the premises, although the buildings are destroyed. It is, therefore, not uncommon for a purchaser immediately to take out insurance against such risks when he signs the agreement of sale. In addition the courts of some states have developed doctrines under which the vendor, if he has insurance, holds any proceeds obtained because of the destruction of the premises for the benefit of the buyer. It is one of the few instances in the law of insurance where two persons can collect for the same damage to the same property.

MODERN TRUSTS AND WILLS

The modern law of trusts arose out of exceptions to the Statute of Uses inherent in the Statute and as interpreted by the judges. The Statute was a response to a dying feudal system and its series of dues and services. Feudalism, for practical purposes, was ended shortly after the death of Henry

VIII, and in 1660 an act was passed to abolish its remnants. In addition Henry died at the beginning of the age of exploration and development which created new wealth and forms of wealth unknown and unheard of in his day.

The Statute itself applied only to "lands, tenements and hereditaments" and therefore did not apply to personal property. Consequently uses, now called trusts, could be created in these new forms of property—stock, bonds, and money in general. In addition the vices of the old use had been, mainly, when the feofee to uses was also the cestui que use, and the feofees to uses had no duties to perform except to hold the property. Consequently the judges formed the rule that an "active" trust, as distinguished from a "passive" or "dry" trust was enforceable even though it was in real property. An active trust is one in which the trustees have management duties to perform—the collection of income and the investment of funds. A passive trust is one that merely conveys legal title and doesn't require that the trustees do anything at all. To this day a passive trust is not enforceable, and the settlor can demand return of the property conveyed, whether real or personal.

Modern Wills

By 1536 the use device had become so commonly employed by the growing mercantile class, in particular, that its abolition caused considerable consternation, for it ended the customary means of leaving land at death in accordance with one's desires. The resulting outcry was the efficient cause of the Statute of Wills (1540) that provided for wills of all socage tenancies and up to two-thirds of military tenures. Upon the abolition of feudalism in 1660, military tenure was abolished and all land became subject to disposition by will.

With the coming of the Industrial Revolution and the corporate form of business in the nineteenth century, vast fortunes of previously unimaginable size came into existence—potent competitors to organized political government. Coupled with the need of government for more and more funds for its various assumed tasks, these fortunes led to a new approach to testamentary disposition of property. Although the right to make a will is undoubted, taxation of estates and inheritances has seriously hampered the transfer of economic power from one generation to another. Just as the income tax has become an accepted and admitted way to redistribute income during life, so death taxes have become a means of avoiding the concentration of economic power in particular families or groups. Our feudal forebears paid relief to obtain their inheritances; we, their successors, pay taxes.

CHAPTER IX

TORTS

The word *tort* comes to us from the Latin *tortus*, meaning twisted or crooked. It came into French, where it still means "wrong." At one time it was used with the same meaning in England, and when the word ceased to be used in everyday speech it continued and found a new life in English law.

Because the term tort covers so many and different wrongs, we can describe what it does but cannot define what it is. What it does is to provide remedies for invasions of rights of person, property, or reputation that are not breaches of contract. The law of torts also provides other procedures, such as injunctions against future violations of rights. This does not tell us, however, the nature of the rights that the law of torts protects. The study of the law of torts, therefore, is a study of those protected rights and of the legal procedures available to protect them.

Torts concern injuries to person, property or reputation. Were there no law of torts an injured person would bear the cost of those injuries. If one were run down by an automobile, injured by a faulty product, or otherwise be subjected to pain, suffering, and loss of bodily function the victim would sustain the cost, both physical and monetary. The slaughtered lamb has no action against the lion. Whether the injury was intentionally inflicted, accidental, or unavoidable would make no difference.

The problem facing courts and legislatures is to determine to what extent, if at all, the cost of injury should be shifted from the victim to the person who, on one theory or another, caused it. It is a prime example of social engineering. As we will see, tort law has developed from a very narrow set of protected rights to one that is very comprehensive, and the widening shows no signs of slowing down. As Professor Simpson wrote in another context, "In the law the winds of change seem to blow in a direction favorable to plaintiffs."

When faced with the question of shifting the cost of injury, lawmakers can choose one of four routes. First, they may do nothing and not shift the cost. Second, they may look to the intent of the person who caused the injury and take the position that if we intend to injure someone we should be liable to the person we injure. Third, they may look for fault. A person, under this theory, should not be liable unless he was, in some meaning of the term, at fault. The fourth is the theory of absolute liability. If one starts a course of action that ultimately results in injury to another person he should be liable. Lack of intention to injure and lack of recognizable fault would be immaterial.

Each of these ideas has a place in modern law. There are areas of harm that the law does not compensate. The law does not expressly say that it will not compensate persons so injured, but has a series of rules that effectively deny recovery, the so-called "no-duty" rules: assumption of risk, contributory negligence, and unforeseeable consequences. It is difficult if not impossible, however, to find a case in which intended injury is left uncompensated. The third approach, fault, or what we now call "negligence," is the dominant theory of modern tort law. Most automobile accident cases, for instance, are brought on the ground of negligence.

Absolute liability is the growing area of modern tort law in the United States. It is the basis of worker's compensation cases and today is applied in product liability cases on the theory that manufacturers should be liable, without regard to intention or fault, for injuries caused by their products.

THE ANCIENT LAW

In tracing the early law of torts, we start with the fact that there was once no differentiation between crimes and torts. Wrongs were first classified as felonies and those that were not felonies. If an offense was punishable by death, dismemberment, escheat, or outlawry, or could be prosecuted by means of the private criminal prosecution known as an appeal of felony (where battle decided the guilt of the accused), it was a felony. If it did not fall in that area, it was one of a vast group of offenses referred to as trespasses or transgressions.

Therefore, said Bracton, "Every felony is a trespass, though every trespass is not a felony."

In this vast group of trespasses, those offenses we would call misdemeanors and those we would call torts were mixed indiscriminately. All these offenses were subject to amercements, or fines, payable in part to the Crown and in part to the injured party.

Undoubtedly, many civil trespasses of a civil nature were redressed in the local and seignorial courts, but with these we have little concern, for they contributed nothing we can easily trace to the growth of the common law of torts.

The Writ of Trespass

As has been noted, in early law the word "trespass" meant "wrong." The word trespass could be applied to many different types of actions that involved tortious civil wrongs. The word trespass did not apply to the older actions. Actions concerning the ownership of real property, and the actions of covenant, debt, and account, were not tortious because they were not based on injury to the plaintiff. Detinue is difficult to characterize because there is a narrow line between suit for what is yours and suing for what you have been deprived. Virtually all other actions could be called trespass, even though that word did not necessarily appear in the name of the writ used to commence these actions.

One of the earliest writs in the royal courts, originally used in King's Bench, was the writ of trespass. Under this writ, misdemeanor and tort were, in actuality, still unseparated. The writ of trespass was based on an allegation that the "peace of the king" had been broken. An early form of the writ, for instance, accused the defendant of having committed an assault and battery against the plaintiff and against the peace of the king. The last phrase gave the King's Court jurisdiction over the civil aspects of the case, which was not a criminal case because words of felony were not used and because the case did not arise by the procedure of indictment. It was a private action. If the plaintiff proved his case, he could recover damages for the assault and battery, and in the same action, the king could impose his fine.

The writ of trespass first appeared around the year 1250 and developed rapidly during the latter half of the thirteenth century. It was a vast improvement over the old Anglo–Saxon *bot,* because it awarded damages fitting the particular case and not based on any set scale of compensation. It was advantageous to the plaintiffs, for they not only procured the relatively impartial justice of the king's judges, but also the great power of the king and his sheriffs to enforce the judgment that was rendered.

The Nominate Trespass Actions

With the passage of time, the writ of trespass was divided into separate varieties which had specific names and therefore are referred to as the "nominate," or named, actions. There was, for instance, the action previously mentioned concerning trespass to the person, called trespass *vi et armis* (with force and arms). Trespass to real property was called trespass *quare clausum fregit* (for breaching the close), and trespass to goods was called trespass *de bonis asportatis* (for taking the goods). The forms were strict, and were applicable to only a limited variety of factual situations.

The Innominate Trespass Actions

Other actions of trespass developed that did not fit within the confines of a specific writ, but were framed to reflect the actual facts of a given case, and therefore varied from case to case. These were called actions of trespass on the case. The phrase "on the case" indicates that the writs were not set forms, but reflected the true facts.

The circumstances that led to trespass on the case (often called "case") are a matter of learned dispute centering about the true interpretation of Chapter 24 of the Statute of Westminster II (1285). That statute was thought, for many years, to have created the authority in Chancery to issue writs of trespass on the case. A later theory was that trespass on the case grew out of trespass as a natural extension. A more modern theory, expressed by Professor Milsom, is that trespass was used in obvious cases—forcible trespasses such as assault and battery and trespass on land—and that case was used in the cases which were not obvious.

The term "case" itself did not, according to Professor Milsom, appear until 1370.

THEORIES OF LIABILITY UNDER THE WRITS OF TRESPASS

One of the easiest and most tempting historical errors to make is to assume that people of an earlier age thought the way we think. Conversely, one of the most difficult historical tasks is to try to determine what people of a prior age were thinking, particularly when they did not explain what they were thinking and all we know is what they did.

Today, the doctrine of stare decisis invites lawyers and judges to think in terms of legal precedents. Members of the profession inspect and dissect prior cases and attempt to determine their underlying concepts and principles, if not detailed rules. The result is an intricate structure of classification and logic that scholars hope can be applied to analyze future factual situations. The danger is that law so devised can, if logic is the dominant goal, be devoid of elementary concepts of justice.

Medieval lawyers could not use that method. There were no judicial opinions in the modern sense. Therefore there could be no doctrine of stare decisis. The juries' general verdicts concealed any discussions the jurors may have had. Discussions in the courtroom were about writs and procedures. The goal of medieval law was to produce a result consistent with reason, and lawyers knew that reason is not a monopoly of the legal profession. Prior cases might or might not have been consistent with reason. If they were, the prior cases added nothing; if they were not, the prior cases were wrong.

As a result a general theory of liability under writs of trespass was not developed, nor even thought about. The goal was a correct decision based on common understanding. Precedents could neither assist one to come to that common understanding nor deter that quest. The result was that each case stood on its own merits, to be decided on the basis of reason alone.

The writ of trespass started to develop in the King's Bench court in the middle of the thirteenth century to cover the civil aspects of obviously wrongful acts such as assault and battery, theft of goods, and unauthorized entry on land. In the royal courts, the oldest of the nominate trespass actions for personal injury, trespass *vi et armis* (with force and arms) imposed liability for acts in breach of the king's peace that caused a direct injury.

Trespasses that were not in breach of the king's peace were heard in the local courts. Local courts heard the bulk of trespass cases. The wrongs remediable in the local courts varied from place to place, because they were whatever local law classified as a wrong. However, by alleging a breach of the king's peace, the plaintiff could gain access to the royal courts. The allegation was omitted if the plaintiff preferred the local courts. The allegation was often untrue, but the royal courts only looked for its presence and did not examine its truth.

By the end of the fourteenth century the royal courts started to hear trespass actions even though they did not allege a breach of the king's peace. Cases might be brought in trespass, usually alleging a breach of the king's peace, or in trespass on the case, without the allegation. Alleging a breach of the king's peace gave the plaintiff the advantage of certain remedies. This fact kept trespass and case as distinct categories even though there was no theoretical distinction and cases, in most instances, could be brought in one or the other.

Because actions in case generally did not allege a breach of the king's peace, court clerks in the sixteenth century started to refer to cases in that way; trespass was against the king's peace and case was not.

The jury in a trespass action would decide whether the defendant was guilty. Essentially, a plea of "Not guilty" meant "I did not do it." The 1617 case of *Weaver v. Ward* added the excuse of inevitability, that the trespass was "utterly without his fault." The jury's verdict did not reveal what the jurors thought, but only their finding.

In the eighteenth century a new theory developed that trespass was for direct injury and case for indirect injury. The famous 1773 case of *Scott v. Shepherd* put to the judges the question of whether trespass was the proper form of action. The judges' opinions on the question was recorded.

In that case Shepherd threw a firecracker into a large crowd. It fell near Willis who, to save himself from harm, threw it away. It landed near Ryal, who also threw it away but this time it exploded in Scott's face and put out one of his eyes. The action was brought in trespass as a battery. Scott chose not to sue Willis or Ryal but to go against Shepherd.

One judge, Justice Blackstone, thought that the injury was consequential, not immediate, and that on a trespass writ Scott could only sue Ryal. He reasoned that Ryal's act, not the acts of Shepherd or Willis, caused Scott's injury. Essentially he thought that the defendant did not do the act that caused Scott's injury, but Ryal did.

The majority disagreed. They thought that Shepherd " * * * was the only person who * * * gave the mischievous faculty to the squib. That mischievous faculty remained in it until the explosion. No new power of doing mischief was communicated to it by Willis or Ryal. It is like the case of a mad ox turned loose in a crowd. The person who turns him loose is answerable in trespass for whatever mischief he may do." The majority thought that the injury was the inevitable consequence of Shepherd's act and was directly caused by his intention to cause "indiscriminate mischief." Disagreeing with Justice Blackstone, they thought that Willis and Ryal were not free agents because they acted under a compulsive necessity for their own safety.

In the meantime actions of trespass on the case were being brought for cases involving what we might call negligence. A smith improperly shoes a horse by driving a nail into the quick of its hoof. Blood poisoning sets in and the horse dies. In the fourteenth century such cases were sometimes brought in trespass, alleging force and arms and a breach of the king's peace, without mentioning the fact that the horse had been entrusted to the smith by its owner. The jury would then find the defendant guilty or not guilty. No reason would be given for the verdict. When the royal courts ceased to require an allegation of force and arms and a breach of the king's peace, the action could simply be brought in trespass on the case, setting out the defendant's alleged fault in terms of breach of duty, negligence, and so forth. Suits in this form could be brought against surgeons, carriers, bailees, innkeepers, and others whose carelessness resulted in injury to their customers' property.

By the eighteenth century the categories had become fairly clear. If an act that resulted in injury was wilful, trespass would lie. If it was not wilful, but accidental, trespass would still lie if the injury was a direct consequence of the act. Fault was immaterial. The defendant caused the harm and was liable. The question was, did the defendant do it.

In trespass on the case fault was the basic element. The plaintiff would set out and prove the nature of the alleged fault. If the jury was not convinced of the defendant's fault, the fact that the defendant did the act that resulted in the plaintiff's injury was irrelevant.

For illustration, take the usual road accident. Suppose there was a collision of two horse-drawn wagons, and the plaintiff's horse was found impaled on the defendant's wagon shaft. In trespass the question would be whether the defendant's wagon struck the plaintiff's horse or whether the plaintiff's horse ran into the defendant's shaft. The first would have been a trespass, the second would not. The question of fault would not enter the picture. To bring it to a modern automobile accident, the question would be who struck whom and not who was negligent.

The plaintiff in a road action could choose to bring an action of trespass on the case. He would then have to allege and prove the defendant's fault. Because this may be difficult, the overwhelming preference was to choose trespass. Procedural rules made it necessary to choose one or the other, and did not permit a case to be commenced in the alternative, trespass or case. If the lawyer chose the wrong form of action the client was out of luck. The case could not be brought again in the correct form.

Although fault was an element in cases of injury to persons or property, it was not an element in cases of taking someone's personal property or invading someone's land. In those cases the nominate writs of trespass were used, and the sole question was, did the defendant take the property or trespass on the land.

NEGLIGENCE

In the nineteenth century, tort law developed differently in England and the United States. Essentially, suits in trespass without alleging negligence were possible in England until 1959.

In nineteenth century United States, the idea of fault as the basis of trespass liability took hold. A leading case decided by the Massachusetts Supreme Court in 1850 involved a dog fight. The plaintiff, in *Brown v. Kendall,* owned one of the dogs and the defendant owned the other. They tried to separate the struggling dogs. The defendant used a stick for that purpose and while circling the fighting dogs raised his stick over his head and accidentally hit the plaintiff's eye, seriously injuring it. The plaintiff sued in trespass and, on the old theory, should have won. It was clear that this event was caused by a voluntary act on the part of the defendant which caused direct injury to the plaintiff. The only old defense would have been that the accident was inevitable, which it was not. Although the court held that trespass was the appropriate form of action, it found for the defendant. It did so on the basis that the only grounds for liability were either that the act was intentional or that it was negligently done.

Chief Justice Shaw's opinion was widely cited and followed in other states. The result was to make the only significance of the distinction between trespass and case a procedural one. A person who was directly injured might bring his suit in trespass, but both trespass and case required the plaintiff to present proof of the defendant's negligence.

The spread of this view was assisted by the movement, which started in the 1840's, to abolish the old and intricate forms of action inherited from England and either to have only one form of action, or to have a few such as assumpsit (for contracts), trespass (for all torts indiscriminately), and replevin (to get back personal property).

Speculation on the reasons for stressing fault liability at that time are not inappropriate, but remains at best mere conjecture. One might observe that it was a hazardous age. People were subject to all sorts of dangers—storms, fires, pestilences, and economic panics. How did these differ from the inevitable accidents of life—being run down by a horse, struck by a falling object, or maimed by an industrial machine? Life was full of natural hazards, and there was no one to go for redress. Why, then, should one collect from another person who was guilty of no fault? From another point of view, why should one have to pay when he was not at fault? Clearly if the defendant

intended harm, or if he could have avoided harm
by being careful, he should pay. But if the act was
unavoidable, perhaps inevitable, the fact that he
was the instrument of its occurrence was unimportant. One authority, Professor Plucknett, suggests
that the meaning of the term inevitable accident
shifted during the nineteenth century from meaning an accident that could not have been avoided
by any means to an accident that could not have
been avoided by any reasonable means. Such an
interpretation is nothing more or less than a reverse way of stating that one is liable if he does not
use reasonable care.

From a litigant's point of view the distinction
probably looked fortuitous or arbitrary. Why
should one be liable in trespass without fault,
merely because the injury was direct and damage
was sustained, but not liable unless there was fault
in an action of case because the injury was indirect
or consequential? Why shouldn't both occurrences
be treated the same way?

Economic thinking may also have played a part.
Home industry was new, and was struggling to get
started. Capital accumulation was a primary
need. A network of roads was starting to be built,
and the science of paving was developing. Railroads were essential in the transportation of goods
and people. To encumber these with a liability
that may ruin a given business because of a fortuitous occurrence was a serious matter. Would people engage in business if they could be wiped out

by a single accident? In the case of employees' claims against employers the courts went even further to favor business. By a trilogy of doctrines they effectively erased, somewhat before the 1850's, the possibility that an employee injured on the job might collect from his employer even if the employer was at fault. In like manner in the 1870's hospitals, schools, and other charitable institutions were granted full immunity for liability from torts. In the area of transportation would people be willing to take to the roads and expose themselves to financial ruin because of something they could not control? Could railroads stand the financial strain of the old doctrine?

The answers to all these questions was that liability should not be imposed merely because one did something, but only if one was in some way at fault in doing it. In accidents in which no fault could be found, the loss would remain where nature put it, on the victim.

As far as personal injury claims against individuals and businesses was concerned, the view was a compromise. Rather than to impose virtual absolute liability, as in the old action of trespass, or to impose a rule of no liability, as was done in the case of hospitals and other charities which were favorites of the courts, a middle course was struck which was to impose liability, but only if fault was shown.

It is important to observe that at that time risk-shifting devices, in other words insurance, were in their infancy. Although fire insurance had long been available, and life insurance was available to persons with money and was soon to be available to the common man through fraternal organizations, casualty and liability insurers were rare. One writer, John Bainbridge, indicates that the first genuine mutual casualty company was the Mutual Boiler Insurance Company of Boston, founded in 1877, and that the first company to issue accident policies was the Franklin Health Assurance Company of Massachusetts, in 1850. In the absence of insurance personal liability is fearsome to contemplate.

MODERN NEGLIGENCE THEORY

The foregoing, of course, merely sets the beginning of a general fault theory in personal injury cases. The concept of what fault was is a separate tale. It came about by taking the general word "negligence," used in the old wording of the writ of trespass on the case, and giving it a technical, legal, meaning. Both English and American cases had a part in the formulation of a meaning for the word "negligence."

An 1883 English case, *Heaven v. Pender,* posed a test that is still valid. It stated the legal question in this manner: "What is the proper definition of the relation between two persons other than the relation established by contract or fraud, which imposes on the one of them a duty toward the other to observe, with regard to the person or property of such other, such ordinary care or skill as may be necessary to prevent injury to his person or property?" The court answered its own question.

* * * whenever one person is by circumstances placed in such a position with regard to another that every one of ordinary sense who did think would at once recognize that if he did not use ordinary care and skill in his own conduct with regard to those circumstances, he would cause danger of injury to the person or property of the other, a duty arises to use ordinary care and skill to avoid such danger.

A more succinct rendering of the same idea is contained in the classic case of *Palsgraf v. Long Island Railroad Company*, decided by the New York Court of Appeals in 1928. In his opinion Justice Cardozo said: "One who seeks redress at law does not make out a cause of action by showing without more that there has been damage to his person. If the harm was not willful, he must show that the act as to him had possibilities of danger so many and apparent as to entitle him to be protected against the doing of it though the harm was unintended."

With fault liability as the major basis for cases involving personal injury, the question came to be whether the defendant owed a duty to the plaintiff. The view developed above in the Heaven and Palsgraf cases did not, of course, apply itself. In one sense the test was whether the defendant could have foreseen the event that actually transpired. Foreseeability is, at best, a vague concept and at worst impossible to apply. Its content has depended on a slow accretion of cases. However because the question of whether a defendant was or was not negligent is ordinarily one for the jury to find the concept of foreseeability is applied differently in different cases.

CONCLUSION

In the totality of tort law, this change to fault liability was only one part of a much larger picture. Its effect was to shift the law, in cases of direct injury to person or personal property, in most cases, to fault liability.

In other areas other shifts took place. Four of them might be used as examples: (1) liability of employers for injuries sustained by their employees on the job, (2) liability for damage done to persons or buildings by blasting, (3) liability of charitable organizations for torts committed by their servants, and (4) liability of manufacturers for personal injury caused by a defect in their products.

As has been noted, early nineteenth century law shifted to a position that, in effect, employers were not liable for injuries to their employees sustained on the job. It did this by the adoption of three doctrines. The first was the ordinary and old doctrine of contributory negligence. If the employee was in any way negligent, the employer was not liable for damages even though he too may have been negligent. Another employer defense was assumption of risk. The employee, in undertaking a dangerous job, assumed the risks of that job. The third was the defense of the "fellow servant doctrine." If the injury occurred because of the negligence of a fellow servant, as distinguished from a superior, the employer was not liable. A primary motive may have been not to burden infant industry with these costs.

With the massive industrialization of the nation after the Civil War, a movement began for the enactment of Worker's Compensation statutes which would make the employer liable for all accidents sustained by employees "in the course of their employment." The warcry of the proponents was essentially economic: "Let the price of the product bear the blood of the workman." It was recognized that the imposition of this liability would increase costs. The thought was, however, that this cost should be spread among all users of the product by increased costs, and not put upon the individuals who happened to get hurt. Industrial accidents are inevitable. Whenever one hears that a bridge is going to be built it is a cause for sadness because we know that the odds are that one or more of the workmen will be injured or lose their lives. Injury, if not death, is equally certain in any industry.

This movement resulted, after 1910, in the adoption of Worker's Compensation in all jurisdictions.

The results have not been catastrophic to industry. One immediate result was the proliferation of insurance companies ready and willing to insure against this new risk imposed upon employers.

In land cases involving blasting, however, the old standard of absolute liability remained fully effective in almost all states. The view was standard that if as a result of blasting, debris or rocks were cast upon a plaintiff's person or property, liability was absolute regardless of the amount of care or skill used in the blasting. The rationale, that was used in other types of cases as well, is that blasting is an ultrahazardous activity undertaken for private profit, and therefore the one who undertakes it should take all the financial risks. It was not dissimilar to the old liability imposed upon those who kept dangerous animals. It was part of the view that, in general, no trespass on land could be excused.

In cases of torts committed by the servants of charities—churches, hospitals, schools, and the like—other policy considerations took hold. Starting in Massachusetts in the 1870's, and spreading to all other jurisdictions, was the view that charities should not be held liable for the torts of their servants committed in the course of their employment, even though other employers were held liable in such cases. The reason given was that these desirable institutions could not exist without that immunity. In the 1870's it was true that much hospital work was done caring for indigent patients, and that hospital income depended largely on the largesse of wealthy individuals. To divert these gifts to payment of claims, rather than to care of patients, would, it was thought, keep gifts from being given. Churches, in this country, also operated on the basis of such gifts, and schools and universities were likewise struggling.

This doctrine continued in full force until the 1960's. Even though by that time hospitals were receiving state funds, and insurance was available for all charitable institutions in wide varieties of coverage, the courts clung tenaciously to the doctrine. Sometimes they invoked the idea that this policy was so imbedded in the law that it required legislative action to change it, ignoring the fact that the doctrine had been judicially imposed in the first place.

The walls of the doctrine crumbled, however, in the 1960's, and the liability of these institutions is now a fault liability, identical to that imposed on business and industry.

The fourth and last area is in the liability of manufacturers for personal injuries caused by defects in their products. When business was in its infancy the problem did not exist. When you purchased an item directly from the producer his liability rested on ordinary contract or tort doctrines.

The advent of the problem came with a developing marketing system—a major component of an industrialized society. The consumer became separated from the producer or manufacturer by any number of persons—jobbers, wholesalers, and retailers. One had one's remedy against the person from whom it was purchased, but what about the more remote parties, particularly the manufacturer?

Here the doctrine of "privity" intervened. Since the purchaser had not purchased the article from the manufacturer he had no privity of contract with him and therefore could not sue him for breach of warranty. In tort the manufacturer was equally immune because he owed no duty toward a person he did not even know.

Except for a few seminal cases, the law in this area started to change after the Civil War. The original breakthrough in this country was on the idea that the manufacturer had a duty of care to a third person purchaser for personal injury resulting in damage if the article manufactured was dangerous to human life because of a defect. However if it was not dangerous, there was no such duty, and the manufacturer's "negligence" in manufacture would not result in liability even though injury resulted. In 1916, in the case of *MacPherson v. Buick,* Mr. Justice Cardozo put the duty this way: "If the nature of a thing is such that it is reasonably certain to place life and limb in peril when negligently made, it is then a thing of danger. Its nature gives warning of the consequences to be expected. If to the element of danger there is added knowledge that the thing will be used by persons other than the purchaser, and used without new tests, then, irrespective of contract, the manufacturer of this thing of danger is under a duty to make it carefully."

During the next fifty years hundreds upon hundreds of cases were brought against manufacturers, some successfully and some unsuccessfully, but in general expanding manufacturers' liability. In the area of foodstuffs, liability was often imposed. One favorite doctrine used to achieve liability was the doctrine of "res ipsa loquitur" which means, freely translated, "the case speaks for itself." If a person is injured under circumstances in which he has not the slightest idea what went wrong, but when all control and knowledge was in the manufacturer or other person sued, it will be assumed that the defendant was negligent unless he can prove he was not negligent. Assume there is a foreign substance in a bottled and capped soft-drink. The plaintiff drinks the contents, not knowing about the foreign substance, and sustains injuries. Because the plaintiff had no idea what went wrong, and all means of control were in the manufacturer, he must explain how he was not negligent. Of course in most such cases the manufacturer had no idea either, so the result was really absolute liability.

Products liability cases of this century are too many and varied to be discussed in short compass, but suffice it to say that the thinking grew that the cost of these events, like Worker's Compensation, were ones that should be added to the cost of the product either directly or through insurance premiums. Just as workers will be injured on the job, so consumers will be injured by products that are defective. The individual should not bear all the damages. They should be considered part of the cost of doing business.

The upshot of the matter was the formulation of section 402A of the Restatement of Torts, Second in 1964. The drafters of that section recommended the adoption by the courts of what amounts to absolute liability on manufacturers for injuries and damages caused by defective products, regardless of negligence or fault. It protects not only purchasers, but any user or consumer, thereby protecting his household, guests, and friends. It applies to any product which is "in a defective condition unreasonably dangerous to the user or consumer or to his property" for any physical harm, as long as the seller is in the business of selling such products and the article is unchanged when it reaches the user or consumer. The exercise of due care is no defense.

This approach is an old answer to a new problem created by an industrial age. It harks back to the old German maxim, that "wer unwillig getan hast, muss willig zahlen," or, "who does something unwillingly must pay for it willingly." Needless to say, the insurance industry has responded mightily to this new liability.

Automobile Accidents and Fault Liability

The mix in the law of absolute liability, no liability, and fault liability is constantly changing. One of the significant developments of the past two decades is the continuing battle between those who favor fault liability in automobile accident cases and those who favor a no-fault system.

Until the early 1970s automobile accident cases were decided on principles of fault liability. The plaintiff had to prove negligence on the part of the defendant. However, if it was found that the plaintiff was also negligent to any degree, and therefore guilty of "contributory negligence," recovery would be denied.

In recent years, virtually all states with fault liability have rejected the doctrine of contributory negligence and have adopted the rule of "comparative negligence." Under that rule if the plaintiff was also negligent his or her damages will not be completely denied, but will be reduced by the percentage the plaintiff's negligence contributed to the accident.

Damages include economic loss, such as medical expenses, rehabilitation expenses, and property damage. They also include non-economic injury, basically the pain and suffering the negligence of the defendant caused to a physically injured plaintiff. Pain and suffering recovery generally exceeds recovery for economic loss by a wide margin. A rule of thumb is that, assuming the plaintiff completely recovers, pain and suffering should be at least four times the economic loss.

The lawyer's mode of compensation in these cases was (and is, in fault liability states) on a "contingent fee" basis. That is, the lawyer agrees to no fee if there is no recovery, but contracts for a percentage of any recovery, usually one-third but sometimes as high as one-half. Assume a personal injury case in which the plaintiff recovers from physical injury completely, and his or her economic loss is $10,000. If the jury finds that pain and suffering amounted to $40,000, the total recovery will be $50,000. Under a one-third contingent fee contract the plaintiff's lawyer is entitled to $16,667, and the plaintiff to $33,333, leaving to one side court costs and litigation expenses. In England, and in western Europe in general, contingent fees are illegal.

A Note on No-fault Insurance

The third party to an automobile accident case is the insurance company. By terms of the insurance policy, the insurance company is required to provide counsel for the defense. Just as the plaintiff's lawyer seeks to obtain maximum recovery, so defense counsel, who are insurance company lawyers, seek a minimum or no recovery.

Only about one percent of automobile liability claims go to court. The others are settled by bargaining. Consequently the amount that may be recovered is unpredictable. Insurance companies are tempted to overpay small claims because the cost of a lawsuit may result in even higher cost. If the claim is large, the need for money to pay expenses may lead the plaintiff to press for an early settlement even though the claim will be underpaid.

Under the fault system, accusations of dishonesty are often made. The lure of a pain and suffering recovery sometimes encourages claimants to magnify their injuries or even to create them out of whole cloth. Attorneys and physicians are accused of collaborating in testimony designed to reflect the client's legal position rather than the physical condition of the plaintiff. Insurance company adjusters, who work out settlements, are sometimes accused of stalling or intimidating the injured party.

One early study found that for each dollar in insurance premiums, accident victims received 14.56 cents to cover "net economic loss" and another 21.54 cents for pain and suffering. Part of the remainder went to pay for economic loss that was already paid for in other ways, such as hospitalization insurance and employer wage continuation plans.

The suggested remedy was to change automobile accident liability from "fault" to "no-fault." No-fault liability means that, in the absence of wilful injury to another or injuries caused by drunken or drugged drivers, the fault or relative fault of either or both parties to an automobile accident is not taken into account. Each vehicle owner would be required to purchase insurance to cover the "net economic loss" of the insured. Litigation between the drivers and their passengers would be eliminated.

Under this plan, medical bills would be paid immediately by the insurance company. Under the original proposal, there was no limit on the amount of these medical payments, rehabilitation expenses, or loss of income. One could not sue for pain and suffering unless the accident resulted in serious and permanent disfigurement, serious impairment of a bodily function, or death. This is known as a "verbal threshold."

As a result, delay, bargaining, underpayments and overpayments, would not occur. The loss would be of the right to sue for pain and suffering. That would be a definite loss to that portion of the bar that specializes in automobile accident cases. Plaintiffs, who by definition do not depend on pain and suffering recoveries for income, would benefit from lower insurance premiums.

When this remedy was proposed to the legislatures of the various states it was heavily opposed by trial lawyers. Sometimes they were successful in defeating the proposed legislation. Sometimes they watered it down to almost complete ineffectiveness by having a provision inserted permitting suits for pain and suffering if medical costs exceeded some low dollar figure, such as $200 or $500. This is known as a "dollar threshold."

As of 1989, fifteen states had adopted some form
of a no-fault system. Michigan has the purest
form of no-fault, but other states have dollar
thresholds for bringing pain and suffering suits
that range from $2,000 to $50,000. Dollar thresholds invite plaintiffs and their lawyers to build up
medical bills to meet the threshold, but Michigan's
verbal threshold, modelled after the original proposal, cannot be evaded.

The law of torts is faced with the problem of how
to allocate the costs of injuries and damages. Insurance distributes costs among the affected population. The theoretical problem is: what costs
should insurance distribute and what costs should
the injured party bear. At the practical level the
problem is whether non-economic loss should be
recoverable at all, or, if it is recoverable, whether
insured persons should be permitted, for a lower
premium, to give up that right.

The law of torts is not static. New developments
create new problems. Sometimes the law is developed by the courts, as in product liability. Sometimes it is developed by legislatures, as in worker's
compensation. Sometimes politics plays a major
role, as in fault and no-fault liability.

The advantage of the United States is that it has
fifty laboratories that can carry out experiments.
A disastrous experiment affects only one state, and
can be undone. A successful experiment, one
hopes, will be copied by other states.

CHAPTER X

CONTRACTS

"Contract" is a word of legal art. It involves the enforceability of a promise or of mutual promises executory in nature, that is, to be carried out in the future. Contract law concerns the elements that make such promises enforceable by the courts.

One must distinguish two types of contracts. The first, a relatively primitive transaction, is a present contract *of* sale. The usual transactions we make every day are examples. One buys a newspaper, or a tube of toothpaste, pays cash immediately, and the transaction is concluded. No promises are usually involved. The second, a sophisticated transaction associated with a trading or commercial situation, involves one or more promises of future performance. I agree, for instance, to buy your house at an agreed price, payment to be made and the deed and possession to be given at or before some specified future date. It is the latter sense of the term contract, a promise *to* sell, with which this chapter is concerned.

In viewing the history of contracts in Anglo–American law, we must also distinguish the formal from the informal contract. A formal contract is a written document, classically under seal; an informal contract may be either implied from the facts of a situation or expressed in speech or writing.

Formal and informal contracts are derived from
different sources. The common, or informal, contract grew out of the writ of trespass on the case,
by a tortuous route. The formal contract is much
older and was born in a day that gave legal significance to solemn acts, particularly when accompanied by some ceremonial element.

EARLY FORMS IN THE NATURE OF CONTRACT

Early royal law was concerned with problems
that affected the central government and not with
purely private disputes. Consequently, by the beginning of the 13th century the royal courts had
jurisdiction over most land disputes and over important crimes. The jurisdiction over land
stemmed from land's importance in the feudal system, and jurisdiction over crime was essential to
an ordered society. The local and seignorial
courts, however, had jurisdiction over usual private
disputes, including what we might call contracts to
sell. Those courts could award damages or dis-
traint against one who did not perform the equivalent of a modern contractual obligation.

Church Courts and Promises

The church courts, partly on the basis of Roman
law and partly on the basis of theology, undertook
to recognize promises solemnly entered into on the
theory that a breach of these promises was a
breach of faith, over which the church claimed

jurisdiction. In church courts a promise, if accompanied by as little as a handclasp, was recognized as binding.

The royal common law courts did not disturb the right of the local courts to hear local disputes that did not involve the interests of the central government. They disapproved, however, of church courts hearing these matters and imposing civil penalties. This was clearly expressed in the Constitutions of Clarendon, in 1164, which restricted jurisdiction over these disputes to the common law courts, the king's justice, whether the transaction was or was not accompanied by a *pledge of faith,* which was a pledge of one's hope of salvation. However, one who untruthfully denied making a promise accompanied by such a pledge was guilty of perjury. Perjury was a moral offense over which the church had jurisdiction. On that basis church courts ordered performance of the promise, which was a way to get around the restriction. Royal courts from time to time issued writs of prohibition demanding that the church courts desist from enforcing such promises. The practice was not fully halted until the 15th century.

Pledges

The early courts came closest to enforcing contracts through the concept of a pledge. If a person made a promise and posted a pledge to guarantee performance, the promisee might forfeit the pledge upon failure to perform. This, however, bears only a vague resemblance to enforcement of the promise itself.

This pledge, then called a "wed" or a "gage," has a few modern remnants. One is that slowly disappearing institution known as the pawn shop. When a person takes personal property to a pawn shop to get a "loan" on it, he does not promise to repay the sum "borrowed." Instead, if he does not repay, the pawn shop operator may retain the pawned item as his own. This was also the original understanding in the mortgage, or "dead pledge." The person borrowing money on the security of real estate would transfer the real estate to the lender, and could receive it back only on repayment of the sum. The law of mortgages has, of course, long been changed. Another remnant is in the traditional Christian ceremony of marriage, in which the bridegroom pledged his honor as security for his promise to care for his wife, whose guardianship was being transferred to him, with the words "and thereto I plight thee my troth."

Each of these should be distinguished from a modern pledge of security, in which the security (for a loan, for instance) that is put up reinforces the promise to repay. The promise to repay is the basis of the obligation.

Common Law Actions in the Nature of Contract

Early judges and lawyers did not think in terms of modern categories such as "contract" or "tort."

They thought in terms of remedies available through the writ system. Some common law writs resemble modern contracts and, as predecessors, supplied some of its elements.

Today, a widely accepted definition of contract is that expressed in Section 1 of the *Restatement of Contracts.* "A contract is a promise or set of promises for the breach of which the law gives a remedy and the performance of which the law in some way recognizes as a duty." The common law writs, however, did not enforce promises in a direct sense, and therefore do not fall under the modern definition. The common law writs that resembled modern contracts were named *debt, covenant, detinue,* and *account.* These writs, beginning with the 12th century, were in use for the better part of five centuries. During this long period they underwent considerable change. Therefore the following discussion is very general.

Covenant.

The word covenant means agreement. To be enforceable under the writ of covenant the agreement had to be in writing. The writ first appeared in the 13th century for the purpose of providing a remedy for lessees against landlords who had breached their duties. A remedy was needed because the possessory assizes only protected freehold estates and a lease for years was not a freehold. At first a successful action against a landlord resulted in the recovery of the unexpired term of the lease. Later, however, damages could be assessed.

From that restricted use covenant came to cover all types of written agreements. If successful, the court ordered the defendant to keep his agreement. If the defendant did not or could not perform the agreement, damages were assessed.

Such agreements were promises to do something in the future, and therefore were similar to modern contracts as defined above. However, by the early 14th century the royal courts required the written agreement to be under *seal*. A seal is any symbol adopted as one's identification. It could be the imprint in wax, attached to the written document, of a person's signet ring which, when rings were individually made, was identifiable. Today a seal can be the word "seal," in parentheses, printed in a place following one's signature.

The seal requirement changed theory. Before the seal requirement the written document was evidence that the parties had come to an agreement. With that requirement, however, the document itself was the agreement. Once the deed (the sealed instrument) was produced and it could be shown that it was made by the defendant, the defendant could not deny the obligation and wage his law against the deed. The defendant could, however, claim that the sealed instrument was defective because, for instance, it was forged, made under duress, or its contents had been misrepresented to an illiterate defendant. Payment could not be pleaded as a defense unless the defendant could produce an acquittance of his creditor, also under seal.

The requirement of the seal meant that the writ of covenant could not be used to enforce informal agreements. Instead, the development of contract law took place in other writs that could enforce informal agreements. This in turn meant that legal thinking took the form of inventing, explaining, and expanding the scope of other writs, and delayed the development of a theory of contracts until the 16th century.

Actions on sealed instruments continue, in some American jurisdictions, to this day. In such cases the contract, called a formal contract, is enforced without regard to the existence of consideration or to the techniques of offer and acceptance. Although it is based on ancient practice, in some cases the sealed instrument performs a useful function. If, for instance, one wishes to bind himself legally to a promise to make a future gift in such a jurisdiction, he need only write: "I promise to pay John Doe $500 on June 1, 2000. (*sgd*) Richard Roe (seal)"

Debt. The earliest writ was the action of debt, probably adopted from prior practice in the local courts. In the time of Glanvill (*c.* 1187) an early and expensive form of the writ was mentioned; in the next fifty years it developed into a rather definite form.

The theory of the action of debt was that a person should pay the agreed price for a benefit received at his request. Suppose A borrowed money from B and did not repay as agreed. He was liable in an action of debt not because of any promise to repay, but because he had received a benefit from B at his request, and the amount of the benefit was a certain agreed sum. It also was used for the agreed price of goods sold and delivered. This was also based on the fact that the buyer, in receiving the goods, had received a benefit from the seller and should pay the agreed price for that benefit; not that he must keep a promise to pay. It was also used to recover rent due from a tenant of land, money due for services rendered, and damages awarded in one of the possessory assizes.

In the very early period an action of debt could be brought in either the local or the royal courts for any amount of money. In the 1290s, however, the rule arose that the royal courts could only hear actions in debt for forty shillings or more. Forty shillings was, at that time, good pay for a year's work.

This did not mean that debt cases for over forty shillings could not be heard in the local courts. Suits in local courts could be started for amounts under forty shillings (thirty-nine shillings eleven pence became popular), but if the suit in debt was for forty or more shillings the plaintiff had to purchase a *justicies* writ from Chancery. The case would be heard in a local court, but the sheriff and not the local court judge would preside. A forty shilling case, therefore, could be heard in either the local or the royal courts.

A claim in the action of debt could be brought on a deed. The deed was the plaintiff's proof of the debt. Or, it could be brought without a deed and the plaintiff's proof was the production of suitors, who were witnesses to the transaction. The plaintiff or his counsel would state his claim in the pleadings and the suitors' function was to substantiate that statement. The plaintiff was not permitted to testify.

A prudent creditor could avoid time, trouble, and risks by advance planning. Many actions in debt were part of the lending process. Suit would be brought against the future debtor in advance of lending money. A judgment for the sum loaned would be obtained, and then the money would change hands.

An even more common practice was for the lender and borrower to go before a court where the borrower would acknowledge the debt and promise to pay it by a certain future day. The debtor also provided that if he did not pay as promised the sheriff could levy on his land or goods. London merchants could use a similar approach after the Statute of Merchants (1283) by appearing before the Mayor of London or some other official where the debt would be acknowledged and enrolled on duplicate records. These were called *recognizances* which is derived from the Latin word for acknowledgement.

Between the suit on the obligation and on an acknowledgement lay the *conditional bond.* Before borrowing money the debtor would sign a bond promising to pay double the amount of the debt if it was not paid by a stated future day. The bond was to be voided, however, if the debtor paid the actual amount of the debt on or before the stated day. The double sum was not considered to be interest (which was illegal in almost all instances) because the borrower could avoid paying the sum by paying the debt on time.

Conditional bonds were also used to enforce formal contracts to submit present disputes to arbitration. The bonds would provide that a party who did not act in accordance with the arbitrator's award would be bound to pay a money penalty. Without the formal bond the arbitrator's award would have had to be enforced by an action in debt. Trial would have been by wager of law, because an arbitrator's decision was not, as it is today, automatically enforceable by the courts.

The action of debt resembles modern contract, but because it did not require the allegation of a promise, did require a "sum certain," and because what constituted a debt differed from county to county, it does not fall within modern contract theory.

Detinue. At the time of Glanvil (c. 1180), debt could be brought for either money or chattels. During the 13th century these two uses became separate forms of action. Debt was used for a demand for money and detinue for a demand for goods that had been bailed to the defendant and had not been returned.

Originally, detinue was based on a bailment (the delivery of temporary possession of goods) and refusal to return. If A, for instance, loaned a plow to B, to be returned at the end of a week, A had an action in detinue against B if B failed to return the plow as agreed. A was demanding the return of his property not the enforcement of a promise. Subsequently, however, detinue would lie for recovery of a chattel even where there was no bailment, and so lost any contractual element it may have contained. Still later it was adapted to recovery of the price due on a contract of sale; but this occurred after the development of modern contract law and may be explained on that basis.

Account. The last of these precontract actions was that of account. Probably developed in the early thirteenth century, it was available against a defendant who had received property from the plaintiff for the benefit of the plaintiff. In that way it can be distinguished from detinue, where the bailment was for the benefit of the defendant. Account was originally the remedy of a landowner against bailiffs who had received money or goods on his behalf. From that point it was extended to lie against agents, partners, and those who held funds for investment. It did not give a remedy, however, against those entrusted with land. To the extent that it required the defendant to return something he previously had promised to return, account had in it some elements of contract. Basically, however, it was founded on the theory of the existence of a formal relationship—bailiff, agent, or partner—which gave rise to a duty to account. A breach of duty, not of promise, gave rise to the action.

The writ of account included an order to the sheriff to require the defendant to produce an account of the plaintiff's money. If the defendant could not prove payment (a jury question) or that no accountable relationship existed (a legal question for the judge), judgment for the plaintiff would order an accounting. To perform the audit, two auditors were either appointed by the judge or, if the defendant was willing to submit to an accounting, by the plaintiff. If the auditors found that money was due the money could be recovered in an action of debt. Wager of law was not available against the auditors' finding because the auditors could, under a 1285 statute, commit the defendant to prison until the sum was paid.

During the 14th century, because of various abuses including attempts to collect trade bills by the writ of account and the use of sham auditors, such as servants of the plaintiff, the right of auditors to commit defaulting debtors to prison was virtually lost. Actions in debt to collect the amount due had to be brought, but the auditors' findings were still not subject to wager of law.

This action died from lack of use as newer contractual remedies developed. Also, the court of Chancery developed an accounting procedure that was much more adaptable to actions against agents and other fiduciaries. Neither wager of law nor jury trial was used and the Chancellor, or masters in Chancery, supervised the accounting procedure. Equity procedures are used to this day to obtain accountings from agents, trustees, and others who hold funds or property on behalf of another person.

Fate of These Actions

Covenant, debt, detinue, and account foreshadow modern contract but were not based on any theory of enforceable promises. For reasons individual to each, they were destined to be superceded or replaced.

Covenant required a sealed document, and this formality made it too cumbersome for use in ordinary mercantile transactions.

Debt was available only when the sum claimed was certain. If the exact amount claimed was not proved the suit would fail. Unless a sealed deed was produced, the defendant could wage his law. Therefore debt could not be brought against the executors of the estates of deceased persons because executors could not wage their law on behalf of a deceased person. In addition, wager of law (except for disputes among merchants) became abused and unpopular. Debt was superceded by modern contract theory.

Detinue also used wager of law. It did not provide a remedy if the chattel was returned in a damaged condition, and the defendant could choose to pay the price of the chattel rather than to return it. It was superceded by a new and more extensive action called *trover*. The theory in detinue was that the defendant had unlawfully detained the property, but in trover the theory was that the defendant had converted the plaintiff's property to his own use.

Account was a complicated and time-consuming action. Its limitation to persons in certain relationships was not conducive to the development of contract theory. As we have seen, it was superceded by another procedure of the same name developed in Chancery.

TRESPASS ON THE CASE ON AN ASSUMPSIT

Although the concepts of trespass and contract appear to be separated by a wide conceptual gulf, they spring from a common source. The word connecting the two concepts is "duty." A basic ingredient of the law of torts is the existence and breach of a duty, and the assumption of a duty is part of every contract. In tort law, duties are socially imposed; but in the case of a contract, the duty is voluntarily assumed by agreement.

The early writs of trespass in the royal courts alleged a breach of the king's peace. This allegation gave the royal courts jurisdiction; without it the case was a private dispute for the local courts. Trespass was for direct and forcible injury. The king's peace surrounded himself, his family, his servants, violence on the king's highways, and during church festivals such as the Easter season. Until 1328 the king's peace died with the king, so that a trespass committed but not tried before the king's death was no trespass.

During the 14th century many cases in trespass were brought alleging a breach of the king's peace in which that claim was clearly fictitious and was made for the purpose of getting the case into the royal courts. Many cases involved blacksmiths, for instance, who were charged with killing horses by force and arms and against the king's peace, when the true facts were doubtless that the blacksmith was what we would call "negligent."

An important case in the early development of trespass on the case was *Bukton v. Townsen* (1348, which has come down to us under the name of the *Humber Ferry Case.* A ferryman received the plaintiff's mare for the purpose of taking her across the Humber River. The ferryman overloaded the ferry. As a consequence the horse slipped into the river and drowned. Chance played a part in the decision because King's Bench happened to be sitting in York instead of Westminster, which was its permanent location. Had King's Bench not been sitting in York the case would have been decided in the local court where the distinction between trespass and covenant was not important.

The action was brought in trespass. Had it been brought in covenant the case could not have been heard in King's Bench, only in Common Pleas.

The defendant argued that the action could not have been brought in covenant because there was none, and that trespass was inappropriate because there was no allegation of the use of force and arms. The judge, however, thought that trespass was proper because of the defendant's misfeasance in overloading the ferry. The plaintiff had alleged an undertaking (an *assumpsit,* or assumed duty) by the ferryman, but the judge declared it a trespass.

Scholars have differed on whether this case was trespass or trespass on the case. The question is not important because the distinction between the two was not developed until later.

Two decades later the royal courts started openly to entertain trespass actions that did not allege force and arms against the king's peace. In 1372 the *Farrier's Case* was brought against a black-smith on a trespass writ based on a plea that the blacksmith had driven nails into the quick of a horse's foot. The court upheld the writ. Other cases were brought against doctors and surgeons for improper treatment, also based on the facts of the case without the ancient allegation.

These cases fell under the heading of *trespass on the case on an assumpsit.* The word "assumpsit" means an assumed duty or undertaking. It was first used in a 1387 case. The basis of assumpsit, which was a tort action, was that the defendant had committed a wrong by, for instance, mistreating an animal or a person. In the middle ages bad workmanship was considered a public as well as a private wrong. Surgeons could be prosecuted for malpractice in the local courts and criminal sanctions could be imposed. In the royal courts, however, such suits were private trespass actions.

Wager of law was not available in actions of trespass on the case. The plaintiff's case rested on the theory that the defendant had not acted in accordance with the standards of his craft, as he was required to do, and that the defendant either had been paid or it had been agreed that he was to be paid. The defense could claim that workmanship standards had been met.

These cases concerned acts that were lawful if properly performed, but that were performed improperly. This is called a *misfeasance,* as distinguished from a *nonfeasance,* which is not doing something. In the 15th century it was established that an action on the case, assumpsit, would not lie for a nonfeasance, or doing nothing. To be sued for doing nothing one would have had to enter a binding promise to do something. A binding promise, however, would have to be made by a written document under seal, and breach of the promise would be remedied by a suit in covenant. The conceptual difficulty faced by 15th century jurists was that to permit a suit in trespass for a nonfeasance, for doing nothing, would have been to permit trespass to provide a remedy for nonfeasance that already existed in the writ of covenant. The rule was that where an older action provided a remedy that remedy must be pursued. The older remedy required a sealed instrument containing the promise, but that requirement concerned proof of the promise and not its essence, nonfeasance.

In the 15th century the duty of the defendant was imposed because he had taken possession or control of whatever was injured. Taking control meant he had assumed a duty of care.

In a later day some thought that the duty of these defendants was socially imposed, and not individually assumed, because they were in the *common callings* on which the law imposed liability for misfeasance. Common callings were occupations or professions in which people held themselves out to work for anyone who requested their services—doctors, surgeons, ferrymen, and common carriers are examples. Whether this theory is true or not is unclear, because in those days common laborers also could, by statute, be hired by anyone at wages fixed by law.

Sales of Goods

A development in the action of debt in the late 15th century also assisted the evolution of the contract idea. The early action of debt required that the buyer actually receive the goods before the seller could sue for the price. The buyer received no benefit, which was the essence of the action of debt, until he received delivery. At that time, however, it was held that title to the goods passed when the bargain (called a *bargain and sale*) was struck even though the seller retained possession awaiting payment. Therefore the buyer received a benefit, title to the goods, at that time. Consequently the seller could sue the buyer in debt for the agreed price, offering to deliver the goods, if the buyer refused to accept them. As a corollary, the buyer could offer payment and bring an action of detinue against the seller if the seller refused to deliver. Having title to the goods, they belonged to the buyer subject to payment of the agreed purchase price.

In the common law courts the passage of title theory did not apply to real property. In theory at least, livery of seisin was needed to constitute and effective enfoeffment. Later in the 15th century Chancery developed the theory that *equitable title* (title recognized in the equity court) passed at the time of the agreement.

Warranties

Today we think of warranties as contracts. We have express warranties, in words or writing and also have so-called implied warranties, which are really imposed by law. We can also treat an express warranty as a misrepresentation made to induce a contract rather than a contract in itself and it then becomes, in equity, the basis for rescission of the fraudulently induced contract.

In the times of which we speak, however, what we call a warranty fell under the heading of *deceit*. Today we think of deceit as a statement the speaker knows to be false, made in the hope that the victim will believe it. But suppose one makes a statement of fact innocently, believing that it is true? From the point of view of the listener the distinction is not important. Whether wilfully or innocently made a loss is suffered. Today the remedy for such a statement is under the heading of *innocent misrepresentation*. The middle ages were not so discriminating. The law was concerned with the result, not the mental attitude of the person making the statement. A deceit was a misrepresentation of a material fact, regardless of the intention of the person making it.

Therefore in the 15th century if one sold goods and gave an express warranty concerning those goods, a breach of that warranty could be remedied by an action of trespass on the case for deceit. This category was separate and distinct from debt and detinue. What words constituted a warranty was a question for the jury.

The express warranty, in the 15th century, was not a contract, but a separate wrong. To treat warranty as a contract would have made the warranty a covenant and its breach a breach of the covenant, or contract. But an enforceable covenant required a seal in the royal courts. Trespass on the case on a deceit, therefore, provided a remedy on the basis that a wrong (which is the essence of trespass but not of breach of contract) had been committed. However, because the intention or fault of the person who made the warranty was immaterial, and because liability for the misrepresentation became absolute, the action although formally for a wrong had a distinct contractual element. It was a wrong only because wrong was essential to an action of trespass, and not because of any actual fault or negligence.

Trespass on the Case on a Deceit

It is from this tortured logic, of finding a wrong where there was none, that the rule developed that, except for the writ of covenant, there was no remedy for a nonfeasance, for doing nothing.

In the latter part of the 15th century the local courts in London began to provide a remedy for nonfeasance through the action of trespass on the case on a deceit. In one case a defendant was sued in deceit in London for selling an entailed estate as a fee. The sale was rescinded and the defendant was imprisoned (a penal sanction for a wrong against the City) until he returned the money received for the land. In another London case a seller who had received the price nevertheless sold to another person. He also was imprisoned awaiting restitution of the price. In London, covenant did not require a sealed document, so an argument that only covenant was available was not relevant.

The best known royal court case of that period was *Doige's Case,* in 1442. The transaction occurred in London. The defendant, for money received, bargained to convey certain land to the plaintiff. Instead, he conveyed the land to a third person. Deceit was alleged. The defendant demurred on the ground that the action should have been in covenant and that there was no sealed document. (In addition, it is not likely that even a sealed document and a suit in covenant would have helped the plaintiff because covenant at that time requested the court to order performance, and the defendant could not perform because he had conveyed the land to the third person.) A full discussion of the issue followed. Plaintiff had judgment on the demurrer.

This case was not one of pure nonfeasance. The defendant did wrong; despite his promise he conveyed the land to a third person. Had he kept the land and done nothing the plaintiff would, under this ruling, have had no remedy. Disabling oneself from being able to perform the contract, therefore, was the deceitful act that gave rise to the case. Contrary to London practice, deceit in the royal courts did not seek restitution of the price but rather consequential damages to be determined by a jury.

Professor Milsom has pointed out a change in thinking that may have taken place when the concept of deceit, as applied in the London courts, was taken up by the royal courts. In the London courts the reason for requiring a disablement to perform, a deceit, was to obtain an order of restitution of the money paid fortified, because deceit was also an offense against the City, by the threat of imprisonment. In the royal courts, however, restitution was not the result of an action in deceit. The remedy was damages as decided by a jury. Consequently, because it became a rule that a disablement, the deceit, was required, pure nonfeasance (failure to convey without a conveyance to another person) was left without a remedy. In such cases lawyers contended that covenant was the only proper action. The fact that covenant would also lie if the land had been conveyed to another person was not germane to the issue. The purchaser's problem was clear: if a conveyance was not essential in covenant, why should it be essential in trespass? To the disappointed purchaser both transactions, with or without the conveyance, were identical. The defendant had not kept his promise to convey.

Other cases closer to pure nonfeasance followed. If a person undertook a task, began it, and then abandoned it to the plaintiff's damage, deceit would lie. For instance, a person agreed to keep a horse for a period of time and then failed to feed it. In one sense this is a nonfeasance, not feeding the horse. In another sense it is a wrongful act, not properly keeping the horse. Without the undertaking to keep the horse the defendant would have had no duty to feed it.

As we have seen, a purchaser who paid for goods had the right to sue the nonperforming seller even though the seller had not sold the goods to a third person. This was a remedy for pure nonfeasance. It fit in with tort theory, however, because the plaintiff-purchaser had suffered a loss, the payment of the purchase price.

Trespass also came to be used, in the 16th century, against persons who did not pay for goods delivered, at their request, to third persons. The loss or detriment to the seller was delivery of the goods to the third person at the defendant's request. In *Holygrave v. Knightsbridge,* a 1535 King's Bench case, Chief Justice Fitzjames presented a hypothetical case. A man wants to buy a piece of cloth and the seller wants cash. The seller does not have the cash. Another man says, "Give him the cloth and I will pay" at a given date. The justice stated that debt would not lie, because the promisor did not receive anything, but that an action on the case would be proper.

Cases in assumpsit were also successful against guarantors of payment. If B sold goods to C relying on A's promise to pay for them if C did not, B had an action against A if payment was not made. A did not request the sale by B to C, but B relied on A's promise in making the sale and his loss or detriment was delivery of the article sold.

As the doctrine that there was no remedy for nonfeasance receded, there remained the basic element that some sort of injury or detriment was needed to bring a case within trespass theory. A *nude pact,* a naked promise without some injury,

was not enforceable at that time except in covenant. Something was required in addition to the
defendant's promise. That something could be the
payment of the price or delivery of the goods.
Passage of title from seller to buyer at the time of
the bargain and sale was a detriment to the seller.
This came to be called the *quid pro quo,* the "what
for what," or "something for something." The
assumpsit, or undertaking, of the surgeon or black-
smith became the way to describe the effect of a
promise. The tort, or trespass, however, was in
breaking that promise. But the promise, to be
enforceable, had to be accompanied by an agreed
detriment.

Part of the stimulus for giving a remedy for
nonfeasance in the common law courts was the fact
that such promises were being enforced in equity,
in Chancery. Oral contracts to convey land for
money, and contracts of guaranty, were enforced
there. Competition for business among the courts
spurred the common law courts to expand their
remedies. To some extent, therefore, the extension
of assumpsit to include cases of nonfeasance was
not a new remedy; it was a way for the common
law courts to attract business that might otherwise
have gone to Chancery.

Theoretically, assumpsit actions in the royal
courts belonged to King's Bench, which had jurisdiction over torts. Actions in debt belonged to
Common Pleas. In practice, however, King's
Bench took jurisdiction over actions in debt on the

fiction that the defendant was a prisoner in the Marshalsea, that court's prison, which gave it jurisdiction over all matters concerning the defendant. This was recognized by a 1585 statute that set up a new court of Exchequer Chamber, consisting of six Common Pleas justices and the Barons of the Exchequer, to hear appeals (writs of error) from King's Bench. The statute apparently approved King's Bench's claim to jurisdiction by specifying the kinds of King's Bench actions to which it would apply: debt, detinue, covenant, and account (which were all traditionally Common Pleas cases, but claimed by King's Bench) as well as traditional trespass actions including the action on the case. In 1573 Common Pleas, in turn, allowed assumpsit to be brought there in lieu of debt. The jurisdiction of the two courts, therefore, in these cases became identical.

Plaintiff's, however, preferred King's Bench. It was quicker, and it did not require the use of serjeants-at-law who had a monopoly in Common Pleas cases. Plaintiff's, of course, decided where the case would be brought.

Up to this point, then, the following picture emerges. First, if a defendant started to perform according to the terms of an undertaking (either as implied by law or as agreed by the parties) and did it improperly (a misfeasance), he was liable in a trespass action. Second, a trespass action would lie against a defendant for nonperformance if he had received something as agreed from the plaintiff which constituted a loss or detriment to the plaintiff. Both of these were based on some loss, injury or detriment to the plaintiff. Third, and on the theory of benefit received, a defendant was liable in debt for nonperformance of a bargain if he had received something as agreed from the plaintiff.

The second and third items seem, indeed, to be reverse sides of the same coin. Both require the defendant to receive something as agreed from the plaintiff. The second, however (the trespass action), was based on the assumption of a duty (an assumpsit) by the defendant via an express promise to perform, while the third (the debt action) was based merely on the theory of receipt of a benefit.

Mutual Executory Promises

The next step was the giant one, to the modern doctrine of the enforceability of mutual executory promises whether or not a direct or out-of-pocket loss was incurred by the plaintiff. This was accomplished through the King's Bench writ called *in-debitatus assumpsit.*

Basically, indebitatus assumpsit was one of the allegations (or counts) within the action of trespass on the case on an assumpsit. Assume an ordinary bargain and sale. P agrees to buy certain specific goods from S at a certain agreed price. Because title passes at the time of the transaction, P has his action of detinue for nondelivery, and S his action in debt for the price if P refuses to accept. To bring the transaction within the assumpsit theory, however, the defendant must have expressly assumed a duty. If, therefore, S sues P for the price he will allege, in addition to alleging the original bargain and sale, a subsequent promise by P to pay the agreed price. The words "indebitatus assumpsit" are significant because they mean, literally, "being indebted, he assumed." This form of action appeared in the middle of the sixteenth century as an alternative to the action of debt.

Toward the end of the sixteenth century King's Bench relaxed its procedure so that although the plaintiff still had to plead the subsequent promise, at trial it was sufficient merely to prove the original debt. A promise to pay was implied when the debt was proved. Common Pleas, however, continued to require proof of the subsequent promise. Therefore the King's Bench action of assumpsit permitted collection of the debt itself, but in Common Pleas it could not be used to collect the debt but rather damages for the breach of the promise, which could differ from the amount of the debt. The debt, for instance, could be the agreed price of goods sold and delivered, but damages from the breach of the promise could be consequential.

As an example, in the 1532 King's Bench case of *Pickering v. Thurgood,* a brewer, for half of the price paid in advance and the other half to be paid on delivery, entered into a bargain and sale with the defendant for forty quarters of malt to be delivered at the time of a certain festival. The defendant then promised delivery at that time. Hoping for delivery, the brewer bought less malt than he otherwise would have, but the defendant did not deliver the malt at the specified time. Therefore the brewer had to buy malt at a much higher price, and his damages were about double the agreed price of the malt contracted for. Judgment was for the plaintiff on the theory that he was wronged by the defendant and had sustained damage because of the failure to deliver. The action was in indebitatus assumpsit and the assumpsit was in the promise to deliver made after the bargain and sale.

Slade's Case

The issue of the need for the subsequent promise came to a head in *Slade v. Morley* (1602). The facts were simple. Slade alleged that at the request of Morley he had bargained and sold to Morley certain grain growing on his land, that Morley had, immediately after the bargain was struck, promised to pay sixteen pounds on a certain day but did not, and damages claimed were forty pounds. The defendant pleaded that the promise was not made in the form alleged.

Slade's Case commenced in King's Bench in 1597. It was agreed that a special verdict should be taken, that is, the jury would not be asked merely who won, which is a general verdict, but would be asked to make specific findings including whether the subsequent promise had actually been made. The jury found that the defendant had bought the grain from the plaintiff, but that there was no other promise or assumption between the parties except the bargain and sale. The jury found damages at sixteen pounds plus twenty shillings for costs.

This special verdict, of course, posed the crucial question. The action of debt clearly could have been brought on the original sale of the grain. The action of indebitatus assumpsit could have been brought had a subsequent promise been made. The jury's finding that there was no subsequent promise raised the crucial issue of whether such a promise was, as Common Pleas maintained, essential to an action in indebitatus assumpsit.

There were at least three discussions before an informal group consisting of all the justices in England and the Barons of the Exchequer. This group was referred to as Exchequer Chamber but was not the court created by the 1585 statute under the same name. It was not a court in the formal sense of a body whose judgments can be enforced. It was a relatively informal meeting at which the judges gave their collective opinion. If this group expressed a dominant opinion no one was likely to contest it.

The defendant strenuously objected to the action on the ground that he could not wage his law in indebitatus assumpsit, but could have done so had the action of debt been brought. The case reports the defendant's claim "that the maintenance of this action takes away the defendant's benefit of wager of law, and thus bereaves him of the benefit that the law gives him, which is his birthright; perhaps the defendant has paid or satisfied the plaintiff in private between themselves alone, of which payment or satisfaction he has no one to testify, and therefore it would be mischievous if he could not wage his law in such case. * * * "

In 1602, after these discussions, the case came up for final decision. The opinion ended with the words that became the foundations of modern contract law:

It was resolved, that every contract executory imports in itself an assumpsit, for when one agrees to pay money, or to deliver anything, he thereby assumes or promises to pay or deliver it, and thus when one sells any goods to another, and agrees to deliver them at a future day, and the other in consideration thereof agrees to pay such a sum at such a day, in that case both parties may have their actions of debt, or actions on the case on an assumpsit, for the mutual executory agreement of both parties imports in itself reciprocal actions upon the case, in addition to actions of debt.

Consequences of Slade's Case

The magic words of Slade's Case were that " * * * every contract executory imports in itself and assumpsit * * *." The subsequent promise was unnecessary. At least four consequences flow:

1. Plaintiffs could sue in assumpsit to recover not only consequential damages but also the debt itself. An action in assumpsit barred a future action in debt, and vice versa. Assumpsit, which had started as a supplement to debt effectively replaced it.

2. It marked the effective end of wager of law, although wager was not formally abolished until 1833.

3. Although displacement of wager of law pleased plaintiffs, because they no longer need fear the defendant's enlistment of compliant oath-helpers, it opened the door to perjured testimony. Consequently, seventy-five years later, in 1677, a statute was adopted, called the *Statute against Frauds and Perjuries,* that required certain contracts to be in writing to be enforceable. These included contracts for the sale of land and contracts for personal property over a certain sum. These provisions continue in the United States in various forms to this day.

4. The civil jury, developed out of the old criminal jury of King's Bench, now dominated common law court cases, except for some surviving ancient actions, such as covenant.

Slade's Case did not answer the question of the liability of executors in assumpsit for contracts of their testators. Executors protested that before Slade's Case the debts of deceased persons were not collectible because their executors, not knowing the facts, could not wage their law. Executors did become liable in assumpsit by 1611.

CONTRACTS IMPLIED IN FACT AND QUASI CONTRACTS

Slade's Case, although momentous from the point of view of future developments, decided a relatively minor point at the time: that a bargain in which the price was agreed was in itself, without a subsequent promise, a sufficient basis for an action of assumpsit. There still remained, however, the problem of the unpaid seller who had delivered goods to another without an express agreement on the price. In such a case, the action of debt would not lie, because no price had been agreed on (no "sum certain"). The action of assumpsit would not lie because there had been no promise to pay. A remedy for this problem developed in the seventeenth century, when the courts started to imply a promise to pay a reasonable price when the buyer, at his request, had received goods or services. This came to be known as a contract *implied-in-fact.*

The courts continued to refuse to enforce, however, an agreement to sell when, in addition to no price having been fixed, the goods had not been delivered. The contract was said to be indefinite and therefore unenforceable, or that it was merely an agreement to agree in the future. In the United States a remedy for this problem was provided in Section 2–305 of the 1952 Uniform Commercial

Code. It provides for the enforcement of a contract for the sale of goods that has no set price "if the parties so intend." The section is known as the "open price terms" provision. It applies, however, only to sales of goods and not to land or services.

There were other situations in which an implied promise to pay was difficult to find, but there was little doubt that the defendant had been unjustly enriched. These included cases imposing liability for money due because of a statute. The defendant had not made a promise; the liability was statutory. The case merely resembles contractual liability and is therefore called *quasi contract* or contract implied-in-law. This was extended to the recovery of money received by a person not entitled to it for a variety of reasons, such as double payment of a debt.

THE DOCTRINE OF CONSIDERATION

A simple statement of what the law of contracts is all about is the short question, "Of all the promises people make, which ones should the law enforce, and why?

Before the development of assumpsit the answer was relatively clear. In the action of debt you were required to keep a promise when you actually received something of value, at your request, in return for it. This was the *quid pro quo* concept. Or, a promise could be enforced in covenant when it was made in writing, solemnly and seriously, and proof was irrefutable. The enforcement of mutual executory promises, however, when nothing had been received, no misfeasance had occurred, and there was only a failure to keep the promise, inevitably raised the question of where the law should draw the line between breached promises for which it should provide a remedy and those for which it should not.

All societies are faced with this basic question. Rome answered it in its highly developed law of obligations. The answer given by modern civil law countries is based on a different theory than that of the United States and England, but even between those two common law countries there are differences.

This basic question is still the subject of spirited debate among the more philosophically inclined members of the academic legal profession. Practitioners, who are primarily interested in winning cases, accept traditional analyses. This discussion is from the practitioner's point of view, and will present the traditional view as developed within the past century or so.

The modern doctrine of consideration has two elements: the price of the promise can be either (1) a legal benefit to the promisor, or (2) a legal detriment to the promisee. The promisor is the person who makes the promise and the promisee is the person to whom the promise is made. A legal detriment is doing or promising to do what one is not legally required to do, or refraining or promising to refrain from doing what one has a legal right to do.

The simplest example is a unilateral contract. Suppose A promises to pay B $500 if B paints A's house white within two months. If B complies, A's legal benefit is that the house is painted. B's legal detriment is in painting the house.

Assume, however, that A promises to give B $500 within two weeks. There is no consideration because A did not receive a legal benefit in return for the promise and B did not sustain or promise to sustain a legal detriment at A's request. There is no promise; merely the promise of a gift. At common law the only way a promise to give a gift was enforceable was if it was made in a written and sealed document, a covenant.

A bilateral contract, in which one party promises to do something or refrain from doing something in return for the other party's promise is more difficult to analyze. In theory the two promises are in consideration for each other. Each party as promisor obtains the legal benefit of the other party's promise, and each party as promisee promises to sustain a legal detriment in return for the promisor's promise. However, the promises of both parties are supported by consideration only if the other party's promise is binding.

Suppose that B, buyer, and S, seller, enter into a bilateral contract to be performed in the future, and that we are trying to find out if B's promise is binding. B's promise is binding only if supported by consideration. That consideration can be S's binding promise. But S's promise is supported by consideration and binding only if B's promise is binding, and that is what we are trying to find out.

Therefore, to find that B's promise is binding we must find, on one theory or another, that S's promise is binding. Some have suggested that the consideration is the promised performance if performance will be a legal detriment to B, as in paying the price, or a legal benefit to S, as in receiving the price, or a legal benefit to B, as in receiving the goods, or a legal detriment to S, as in delivering the goods. If this is true, why do we not merely say that mutual promises are binding? The reason is that saying so would bring us back to the basic question, what promises are binding? Basically, whether or not the promisee sustains or promises to sustain a legal detriment in return for the promisor's promise determines the enforceability of that promise.

The problem of legal detriment is the despair of theorists. Some use the term without defining it, and others do not use the term, preferring to speak of "sufficient consideration." Reduced to its simplest terms, the problem is to define those transactions that we can assume the parties intended to be legally binding, or that should be binding if injustice is to be avoided. Such a definition, because of the infinite variety of possible transactions, cannot be formulated.

The stress on benefit and detriment has led some legal historians to look for the origins of the doctrine of consideration in older law. Some have analogized the action of debt, which required a quid pro quo. The quid pro quo in debt was some benefit to the defendant bestowed on the plaintiff.

It has also been suggested that the idea of legal detriment inhered in the action of assumpsit, which developed out of trespass theory. They reason that the plaintiff's reliance on the promise resulted in an injury, or detriment.

Concerning the first argument on the writ of debt, it is true that many assumpsit actions pleaded that the promise to pay was "in consideration of" the antecedent debt. However, the antecedent debt was the motive or reason for the promise to pay, not the benefit that gave rise to the action of debt. In modern consideration analysis, the antecedent debt could not be consideration for the subsequent promise to pay, for that would have been a promise to do what one was already legally bound to do, and therefore would not be a legal detriment. The antecedent debt was a reason or motive for the later promise, but could not have been in return for the later promise.

Concerning the second argument which analogizes the action of assumpsit, one can note that although the action of deceit required injury or damage, the action of assumpsit did not. One commentator has suggested that the second promise restrained the plaintiff from bringing an action in debt, and that the breach of the second promise therefore was an injury to the promisee because that promise had induced the plaintiff not to exercise his right to sue in debt. This suggestion, although ingenious, is conjectural and finds no support in the cases. The plaintiff did not give up or promise to give up his right to sue in debt. Even after the subsequent promise was given he might have chosen to sue in debt. His choice of assumpsit was a voluntary surrender of the right to sue in debt. The subsequent promise gave the plaintiff an option he previously did not have.

A more likely source is in the court of Chancery which, in cases involving uses, referred to the causes or considerations of those transactions. Money, services, marriage, and even love and affection were considered good considerations.

The earliest American casebook on contracts, by Christopher Columbus Langdell in 1871, reports a few early English cases on consideration. The first is *Smith and Smith's Case* in Queen's Bench in 1583, an action on the case that stated that " * * * here there is not any benefit to the defendant that should be consideration in law to induce him to make this promise * * * * " In a 1595 case it was held that payment of a lesser sum to discharge a larger debt was supported by consideration because " * * * it is a benefit unto him to have it without suit or charge * * * * " (It should be noted that this is no longer the law. The defendant's promise to pay a lesser sum than is due is only a promise to do what he is already bound to do, and therefore is not a legal detriment.) In a case in 1600, it was stated that although love and affection were not sufficient consideration at common law, a promise to pay for board supplied to a son was supported by good consideration.

These and similar statements do not, of course, present a full-fledged doctrine of consideration. They do, however, contain the seeds of the doctrine. The first two cases recognized benefit to the promisor as a sufficient consideration, and the third case recognized a promise to sustain a legal detriment as a sufficient consideration.

The most eminent mercantile judge of the eighteenth century, Lord Mansfield, would have limited the requirement of consideration to contracts that were not in writing. To him, consideration was evidentiary and was needed only to show that a contract had been made. If the contract was in writing, he maintained, the agreement was binding without more. Except, however, for a few specialized promises, such as to pay a debt that had been discharged in bankruptcy, his view did not prevail.

The technical requirements of modern contract law were developed in the late nineteenth and early twentieth centuries. Blackstone in 1756 and Chancellor Kent in 1826 barely touched the subject of contracts. Before the advent of commerce and industry mercantile law was not nearly as important, nor as intricate and interesting, as the law of real property. By 1871, however, Langdell's "Cases on the Law of Contracts" devoted a fourth of its one thousand pages to consideration. Oliver Wendell Holmes, Jr., in his classic 1881 "The Common Law," devoted three of his eleven chapters to contracts. 1920 saw the beginning of Samuel Williston's massive treatise on the law of contracts. Because the construction of an integrated theory requires interpreting cases, filling in gaps that the cases do not fill, and ignoring cases that do not fit within the proposed theory, it can be said that the theorists made as much law as they found in the cases.

As law schools replaced apprenticeships as the primary means of legal education, generations of lawyers and judges were indoctrinated with this academic learning. In recent years criticism has been heaped upon this inherited dogma; some have even declared contract to be dead.

Criticism of the doctrine of consideration is based on the fact that many cases have held promises binding even though no consideration could be found. Upholders of the classic dogma claimed that such cases were aberrations, or wrongly decided. Another theory, however, goes a long way toward explaining them. The theory is of justifiable reliance on a promise that results in injury if the promise is not kept. It is a revival of the ancient concept of a tort. Contract theory, with its requirement of consideration, created a new category out of its tort background. The reliance theory, however, brings contract back to the basic tort concept of injury.

In American contract law, the reliance theory comes under the general heading of "promissory estoppel." The idea of estoppel is simple. It is that if one person, by some act or promise, knowingly induces another person irretrievably to change his position, the first person will be held to the promise. In the law of contracts it means that if one person makes a promise that he knows, or reasonably should know, the promisee will rely on in some material way, the promise will be binding if injustice can only be avoided by enforcing the promise. Formal consideration, a legal benefit or detriment, is not needed.

The doctrine of promissory estoppel was first applied in non-commercial situations, such as promises of gifts to charities. It now applies to commercial transactions as well.

ECONOMIC FORCES

In this survey of the development of contract law we have traversed a period extending from the beginnings of the English common law to the twentieth century. The need for contracts is a need of a commercial, not an agricultural, society. When commerce was of relatively little importance, when the manorial system was the productive pivot of society, there was little need for enforcement of mutual executory promises. The ancient actions of debt and covenant, and the law of merchants enforced in periodic fairs, in the staple cities, and to some extent in the borough courts, were quite sufficient to meet the economic needs of society.

The press of cases which provided the occasion for the development of contract law began in the fifteenth century, became considerably stronger in the sixteenth century, and resulted in a virtually complete legal response in the seventeenth and eighteenth centuries. This evolution coincides almost exactly with the breakdown of the manorial system in England and the development of a mercantilist, and subsequently capitalist, economic system.

Although the manors had been virtually self-sufficient economic entities until the thirteenth century, that period saw the timorous beginnings of the enclosure movement, a tendency of landlords to make their own sheepwalks from common land previously available for pasturage. Trade was increasing, and wool was a profitable item of commerce. The enclosure movement was followed in the succeeding centuries by the abandonment of the traditional organization of agriculture. Tenants were forced off the land into the growing cities, in order that a more advanced organization of agriculture might take the place of the ancient manor—all this occurred in search of the money needed to satisfy the increasing demands of the propertied classes.

This in turn created a reservoir of labor pressing for employment in the cities and towns, employed by a new class of manufacturers whose competition with the older guildsmen resulted, ultimately, in the creation of a new economic order. Feudalism, which had started as a military system and then had changed into a social system based on the ownership of land, was destroyed by extensive trade and manufacturing, new modes of producing wealth. For these the development of contract law was essential.

The law of contracts was a response to economic change. The focus of the law was to enforce bargains, and the exchange of values inherent in a bargain is the essence of the doctrine of consideration.

Until the twentieth century, most change was accomplished by courts and rationalized by theorists. Fashioned in this way, and bound by the chains of precedent, the common law method became incapable of keeping up with the times. The result was legislation, which in the United States is exemplified by the Uniform Commercial Code of 1952 and its amendments. The Code applies only to sales of goods and securities, and not to land transactions. Therefore the law can differ depending on whether land is the subject of the transaction.

Changes reflect changing business practices and expectations. At one time an option, which is a promise to keep an offer open, had to be supported by consideration. Today a gratuitous promise of an option is enforceable. At one time any change in an existing contract required consideration. To-day a consensual change is binding without more if it is made in good faith. Many Code provisions validate agreements made in accordance with commercial standards, without regard to legalistic formalities. Lord Mansfield, who gained many of his insights on commercial practices by frequenting eighteenth century coffee houses enjoyed by merchants, would have agreed.

PART IV

THE COMMON LAW CODIFIED

CHAPTER XI

THE LAW AND COMMERCE— ACTION AND REACTION

Although the common law has always responded to the pressures of society, in no area is the effect of that pressure quite so clear as in commercial law. Commercial law includes the law concerning transfer of rights in personal property (the law of sales) and intangible rights to sue (the law of assignments and commercial paper), the law of business organizations (partnerships and corporations), of business representation (agency), of shipping, and of insurance.

Trade can exist only when society reaches a stage in which some areas have surplus production and other areas are in need of that surplus and have something to offer in exchange. Then there must be a means to transport goods from one place to another and persons willing to engage in that endeavor. So long as a given society is basically agricultural and self-sufficient, trade finds an insignificant place. When a society starts to become urbanized, however, the stage for commerce is set, for rarely can all the needs and wants of the citizens be met locally.

From that point, the development of trade depends upon conditions favorable to traders: roads and ships, a medium of exchange, a system of commercial rules or laws. There must be standard weights and measures, a system of credit, and devices for accumulation of capital. Agents become necessary for representation, and everyone must work in an ethical climate that favors trade and provides some political stability.

EARLY MERCANTILE LAW

These conditions have existed at many times and in many places in the Western world. One of the earliest known trading civilizations developed on the Mediterranean island of Crete before its destruction about 1500 B.C., perhaps by the eruption of a tremendous volcano on the nearby island of Thera. Strategically situated in the Mediterranean, as an island it was virtually immune from invasion and yet no more than a few days voyage by sea from the land masses of Europe, Asia Minor, and North Africa. More is known about Ancient Greece which was acquainted with trade, but which never developed trade significantly, partly because of its basic political instability and unwillingness to develop foreign markets as sources of supply.

Rome developed trade to a much greater extent, but the position and prestige of traders was never sufficiently high to give them influence in the formation of the law. Such influence is essential if more than the rudimentary needs of trade are to be met by a legal system; for if groups inimical to traders formulate the law, it is highly unlikely that the law will reflect the needs of trade.

This theory can be supported by examples of communities with favorable legal climates. Rhodes, a community largely dependent upon trade, created a basic law of the sea during the third and second centuries B.C., which many subsequent codes followed, and sea-law for the next one thousand years was known as Rhodian law. After the conquest and decline of Rome, merchants in Italy and southern Europe often obtained control of the governments of cities, and each of these towns created its own basic laws of commerce. Amalfi, near Naples, had such a code in the eleventh century, and Barcelona in the twelfth. Oleron, an island (then owned by England) in the Bay of Biscay, also had such a code in the twelfth century. The codes of the Mediterranean area were compiled in the fifteenth century into a collection known as the *Consolato del Mare*, which became dominant in that area.

A different approach was followed in the north of Europe. Rather than through overt control, as in the southern cities, the power of merchants was expressed through franchises obtained from gov-

ernment, which entitled merchants to create their
own rules of law and to enforce these rules through
their own courts. Franchises to hold fairs were
temporary; but the franchises of the staple cities,
empowered to deal in certain basic commodities,
were permanent. Because Italian law had developed earlier than the law in northern Europe, the
northerners modeled their own law after it. Consequently there arose the laws of Wisby, and those
of the Hanseatic League (which was in existence
from the fourteenth to the seventeenth centuries).
By the beginning of the modern period of trade
expansion, the dominant codes were those of Oleron, Wisby, the Hanseatic League, and the *Consolato del Mare.*

Although Roman law provided a theoretical
model for the development of these codes and although many of its concepts were adopted and
followed, in specific details the Roman law concerning trade was not as highly developed as the
city codes of the seventeenth century. In fact, the
attempted revival of Roman law in Italy during
that time may have postponed the development of
modern rules in some areas of law.

English commercial law followed northern European practices, but based on the laws of Oleron.
Commercial law was used in the franchised courts
of the fairs and in the separate courts of the
boroughs. Many trading towns had their own ad-
aptations of commercial law, such as the Oak Book
of Southampton, the Red Book of Bristol, and, with

the creation of an Admiralty jurisdiction, the Black Book of the Admiralty.

The seventeenth century movement toward national governments resulted in a decline of separate mercantile franchises and their courts. The staple towns, for instance, had outlived their usefulness. When the law merchant became incorporated into a national system of laws enforced by national courts of general jurisdiction, the local codes were finally extinguished. But national systems of law necessarily depended upon the older codes for their stock of ideas and on the changing customs of merchants for new developments.

THE DEVELOPMENT OF TRADE

From the fall of Rome until the eleventh century, there was little trade in Europe. The first post-Roman revival of trade came about in the eighth century through the efforts of the Arabs, followed by the Lombards, who were the first European trading group to bring commerce to all of Europe, including England. The Crusades introduced Europeans to the exotic products of the East, and the resulting demand further stimulated trade.

English trade was dominated by aliens until the late fourteenth century. The manorial system, virtually self-sufficient, started to break down after the Black Death (1348–1349), and the subsequent growth of towns with a surplus of labor led in turn to the dissolution of the restrictive guild system and the growth of an indigenous merchant class with demands of its own. Ultimate political representation of the middle class in the House of Commons and the passage of legislation to spur commerce created a favorable climate for mercantile development. Commercial practices were significant in creating the common law, a fact that was recognized by important judges who led the way to complete integration of the two.

Commercial law is the story of the confrontation of the common-law courts and the trading community. England was ceasing to be an agricultural community and was emerging as the dominant trading center of the world. The common law could not permit commercial law to continue to develop along independent lines, but it was unable fully to conform to business needs. How an accommodation was accomplished in the areas of negotiable instruments and business organizations will next be considered.

CHAPTER XII

NEGOTIABLE INSTRUMENTS

The widespread laws of merchants are commonly referred to as the *lex mercatoria,* or law merchant, and may be divided into two parts: admiralty law, dealing with maritime commerce, and commercial law, dealing with commerce ashore. Space forbids dealing with maritime law; the parts of commercial law here considered are the law of negotiable instruments, partnerships, and corporations.

TYPES OF NEGOTIABLE INSTRUMENTS

There are two basic negotiable instruments which, although they have totally different purposes, have three indispensable features in common. The first is the promissory note, an evidence of indebtedness. It states that one person, the maker, owes money to the other, the payee. The second type is an order to pay, called a draft, or, earlier, a bill of exchange. One person, the drawer, orders another, the drawee, to pay a certain sum of money to a third person, called the payee. The most common example is the simple bank check.

The three features these instruments share are: (1) they are readily transferable (negotiable) from one person to another, (2) the ultimate holder can

261

sue on them in his own name, and (3) the ultimate holder for value and in good faith takes good title to a genuine instrument free of prior defects. Two examples may suffice.

1. A maker signs a promissory note payable to the order of a payee in return for the payee's promise to deliver goods in the future. The payee negotiates the note to a holder, who is a good-faith purchaser for value, but the payee does not deliver the goods to the note's maker. The holder demands payment from the maker, who defends on the ground that the promised goods were not delivered. The maker's defense, although good against the payee, is futile. He must pay the holder.

2. The same result would follow if, instead of giving the payee a note, the purchaser drew a check on the drawee bank to the payee's order, and the check came into the hands of a good-faith holder for value.

It is important to keep in mind that an instrument payable to a named payee only, without mentioning another possible holder (by adding the words "or order" or bearer after the name of the payee) has never created a fully negotiable instrument. The three features mentioned do not apply to a nonnegotiable instrument.

The promissory note and the draft, commonly treated together today, are the result of different although related lines of development; therefore, they will be considered separately.

THE BILL OF EXCHANGE, OR DRAFT

The bill of exchange, now commonly called a draft, is a basic and essential commercial instrument. When merchants deal with one another, respective debits and credits arise. These can be settled by the transfer of money, but apparently every trading group that has ever developed considerable trade has found it more advantageous and considerably safer to settle accounts by means of some commercial document similar to the draft.

Suppose, for instance, that A, a medieval French merchant, desired to purchase goods from B, a merchant in Italy. A might, conceivably, have sent payment to B in coin or bullion in the custody of a servant. But it would have been much more convenient for A to go to another French merchant, C, who had a credit with another Italian merchant, D, and have C prepare a document ordering his Italian merchant debtor, D, to pay the needed sum to B.

These were the parties to the original bill of exchange: A, the purchaser, B, the payee, C, the drawer, and D, the drawee. Notice that there were four parties to this transaction instead of the three parties to the modern draft.

Early Enforcement

This device appeared as early as the fourteenth century in Europe, and it was used in England in the sixteenth and early seventeenth centuries. It

developed out of an even earlier procedure involving the use of agents. Since much medieval trade
took place at the periodic local fairs, merchants
often arranged to settle their accounts there.
Their agents would go to the fair armed with
documents authorizing the settling of their respective accounts. Since the fairs were used by merchants from numerous places, they became large
clearing houses for the debts of European merchants. The fairs were essential to medieval trade,
and only after the sixteenth century were they
superseded by more modern marketing devices.

In all parts of Europe, until the nationalization
of law in the seventeenth century, these instruments were enforced in special merchants' courts.
In England, courts frequented by merchants were
of various types: the courts of the fairs, those of
the boroughs, of the staple cities, and the Court of
Admiralty (which began in the fourteenth century,
but the records of which are available only from
the middle of the sixteenth century). Courts of the
fairs and boroughs dealt with domestic trade, while
those of the staple cities mainly governed foreign
trade. The position of Admiralty varied through
the years of its existence, until its jurisdiction over
commercial matters, as distinguished from maritime matters, was taken over by the common-law
courts in the middle of the seventeenth century.
By that time, fairs were virtually obsolete, and the
monopoly of the staple cities over foreign trade was
at an end.

The courts of the boroughs and fairs were important in the development of negotiable instruments until the seventeenth century, when the common-law courts took over this jurisdiction. Fairs usually were held by lords or churches, but sometimes they were held in boroughs. The franchise to hold a fair included the right to hold a court there. These courts were referred to as the Piepowder courts, probably derived from *pieds poudres,* or the dusty feet of the merchants. Their temporary nature necessitated speedy justice. All sorts of offenses were tried in them, including forestalling (attempting to raise prices by artifice), use of false measures, theft, assault and battery, interfering with a sale, defamation of credit, breach of express warranty, failure to deliver in accordance with samples, and the like. One interesting feature of these fairs was that a good-faith purchaser of goods in such an open market (called a market overt) obtained good title to the goods, despite the fact that they might have been stolen previously.

Borough courts were concerned with domestic trade of a continuing nature; and since boroughs were also the centers of guilds, they were involved with problems concerning apprentices and the liability of merchants for contracts of their agents. If foreign merchants were the litigants, a jury of foreign merchants was used; if one party was English and the other alien, the membership of the jury reflected an equal division of origin. Market law was a small although significant part of borough law.

By the fifteenth century, English foreign trade was coming into the hands of English merchants who, quite naturally, adopted the Continental bill of exchange developed mainly by the Italians. It appears from a few fragmentary records that these documents were recognized in the Court of Admiralty and the Mayor's Court of London, but there were no cases in the common-law courts until 1602. By that time it was fairly well established on the Continent that bills of exchange were enforceable and transferable by endorsement.

In Common–Law Courts

The common-law courts had great difficulty handling these instruments. Their forms of action were not well suited to them—they had to work through the action of assumpsit in order to give relief. The purchaser of a four-party bill of exchange theoretically could easily sue the drawee if he did not pay the bill, on the theory of injury by reason of the drawee's failure to live up to his undertaking. Problems arose, however, when the payee desired to sue a drawee who refused to pay the bill of exchange because the payee had given the drawee no consideration for his promise to honor the bill. (The consideration moved from the purchaser of the bill.) In order to get around that difficulty, it was alleged that the payee was the agent of the purchaser of the bill of exchange when the purchaser obtained the bill from the drawer, originally. Thus, for the purpose of finding consideration, the purchaser and the payee were one party. The purchaser purportedly paid for the bill of exchange on behalf of the payee. This, of course, was total fiction.

Introduction of Law Merchant to the Common Law

Such tortuous maneuvers obviously could not long continue if the law was to develop, and the common-law courts therefore turned to the device of permitting the writ of assumpsit to be issued in accordance with the custom of merchants. This required that the alleged mercantile custom be set forth in detail in the pleadings, and then that its existence be proved at the trial. By 1666 it was declared that the law of merchants was part of the common law of England, and therefore need not be specially alleged. It came to be the rule that the proof of a custom of merchants adopted in one case would make that custom part of the law, so that it need not be proved in a subsequent case.

By 1651 the modern three-party bill of exchange (drawer, drawee, and payee) was in use, and it could be payable either to the "order of" or to the "assignee of" the payee. A bill of exchange payable to bearer could be created by leaving the name of the payee blank (rather than by the modern usage of making it payable expressly to "bearer"). This adoption of the custom of merchants created an exception, for these mercantile instruments, to the common-law rule that a contract right could not be assigned.

Assignments At Common Law

Two difficulties lay in the way of permitting the transfer of an obligation from a creditor to his assignee. First, a debt was deemed to be personal. This concept had much merit in a day when a creditor could imprison his debtor for not paying a debt. Although a debtor's original creditor might be a tenderhearted man, not given to such harsh treatment, his assignee might be a merciless person who would put the debtor in prison without compunction.

Second, the common law could not see that there was anything to transfer. Goods of all types could be sold and transferred because they were the subject of manual delivery. A right to sue, however, as a mere intangible "chose in action," had no material substance and therefore was deemed incapable of transfer. The paper which reflected the contract was tangible, to be sure, but it was mere evidence of the right and not the right itself. (If, for instance, a contract is destroyed by accident, the right it evidences still exists, although it may be more difficult to prove.) This stress on physical form was important to the common law until very recent times.

The custom of transferring negotiable instruments by endorsements was established among merchants, nevertheless, by the seventeenth century. When the law came to the point of recognizing merchant customs, it recognized such transfers by endorsement but still denied a transfer of a contract right in transactions not within mercantile custom.

By the middle of the seventeenth century, therefore, a bill of exchange could be transferred from one party to another by endorsement, and the holder could sue on it in his own name. These accomplishments were made possible by common-law adoption of the customs of merchants.

Although two elements of modern negotiability had been settled, the courts still were reluctant in the middle of the seventeenth century to give the transferee of a bill of exchange better title to it than was held by his transferor. The instrument might be subject to such defenses, for instance, as failure of consideration, or that it was given in payment of a gambling debt.

The first case freeing a good-faith holder for value from a defense valid against the payee was decided in 1699. There it was held that one who lost a bill of exchange could not retrieve it once it fell into the hands of a good-faith holder. With this decision we reach the beginning of the modern development of the bill of exchange.

PROMISSORY NOTES

The ancestor of the modern promissory note is the old "writing obligatory," a document earlier than the bill of exchange, although its successor, the promissory note, received recognition in English law at a later date.

The earliest writings obligatory were of two types: (1) formal documents under seal, and (2) an informal variety, not under seal. The formal document was recognized at common law through the action of covenant, but the informal type was not recognized as valid.

By the seventeenth century the sealed writing could, on the Continent, be made payable to one's creditor or to the bearer. In England, however, such a writing was payable only to the creditor or his attorney-in-fact. The creditor, therefore, might transfer the document to another, but that person would have to sue as the creditor's agent and therefore would be subject to all defenses good against the creditor. He could not sue in his own name, and he would not get a better title than his predecessor had. Some of these documents were payable to the creditor or the "producer" of the document, apparently in an attempt to create bearer instruments, but their validity in the hands of such a producer is questionable.

Importance of the Goldsmiths' Activities

The forerunners of bankers, goldsmiths were largely responsible for increased use of informal writings obligatory, or promissory notes. Insecurity during the Civil War and the period of the Commonwealth and Protectorate (1649–1660) led people to entrust their gold to the goldsmiths rather than keep it in the form of plate or in the Tower of London, as had been the custom of many. The goldsmiths lent this wealth at interest to the government and to merchants and paid interest to their depositors. The deposits were evidenced by promissory notes. Goldsmiths also started to pay their depositors' debts, on request, using the money left with them.

A few cases involving such promissory notes were heard by the common-law courts in the latter half of the seventeenth century, but no clear trend toward negotiability was apparent. In *Clerke v. Martin* (1702), furthermore, a dictum maintained that they were not negotiable. It stated the unfortunate opinion that although a bill of exchange was transferable because of the custom of merchants, a promissory note, whether to order or in the form of a bearer instrument, was not negotiable. This point was confirmed in 1703.

That decision, by Lord Holt, was based on the idea that promissory notes were new inventions of the goldsmiths and should not be permitted to create law for the courts. Lord Holt thought that the goldsmiths might have achieved their object by drawing a bill of exchange to the order of the drawer (as one makes out a check to himself to obtain cash) and therefore that the promissory note was not commercially essential.

The Statute of Anne

These opinions resulted in the first direct legislative interference in the course of negotiable instruments law. Although the aptness of Lord Holt's decision is the subject of scholarly controversy, it seems clear that the decision was contrary to the needs and legitimate demands of merchants. The Statute of Anne (1704) consequently was enacted to confer negotiability upon promissory notes, so that a transferee could sue the maker, on either order or bearer instruments, in the manner of bills of exchange.

SUBSEQUENT COMMON LAW DEVELOPMENTS

Until the time of statutory codifications in the late nineteenth century, the history of negotiable instruments is one of gradual refinements, culminating during the tenure of Lord Mansfield (1705–1793), Chief Justice of the King's Bench from 1756 to 1788. Mansfield was particularly qualified for the task of redefining commercial law because of his background and predispositions. As a Scotsman he was interested in, and learned in, Scottish law, which was based on the civil law principles so basic to Continental mercantile law. As an individual, he was inclined to seek advice from merchants concerning mercantile practice and to adopt it as the law. In cases in which the law was in doubt, evidence of mercantile custom was admitted, and Mansfield used merchants on his juries.

The basic conflict to be resolved was one between justice and certainty. An approach to absolute justice would have required that mercantile custom be considered in each case, in order that it might reflect alterations in practice. Certainty, at the opposite end, would require the law to consider no custom. Mansfield's compromise was to admit custom into evidence where the law was uncertain; but once a point was settled, to exclude evidence of custom thereafter. The first case decided the law.

His primary contribution was in the refinement and definition of terms and the rights of parties. To the sparse comments of prior cases he added analysis, reason, and logic. Although it had been decided in 1699 that a good-faith holder for value of a bill of exchange had rights superior to one who lost it, Mansfield gave form and logic to the point in *Miller v. Race* (1758) whence the doctrine is often traced. Another such refinement was the famous case of *Price v. Neal* (1762) holding that a drawee cannot regain the money he has paid out on a forged bill of exchange. The liabilities and rights of the parties to negotiable instruments were thus settled by a series of decisions during Mansfield's tenure.

THE CODIFICATION MOVEMENT

Further refinement of unsettled points took place both in England and in the United States up to about 1875. By that time, the accumulated mass of decisions appeared to cry for simplification. In this country, the problem was complicated by the fact that the different states had developed different answers to some of the same problems.

The French had organized negotiable instruments law by an ordinance in 1673, perhaps at too early a state of development. This ordinance, expanded, was incorporated into the French Code of Commerce in 1818.

The codification movement in the area of negotiable instruments started in England. In 1878 Sir Mackenzie Chalmers published his *Digest of the Laws of Bills of Exchange,* distinguished from several prior works on the topic in that it was a series of 287 propositions. The form may have derived from Chalmers' acquaintance with prior eighteenth century codes in British India, where simplified statutes were essential because India had no background of case law on which to rely.

In 1881, Chalmers presented to the British Institute of Bankers a paper on the advantages of codifying the law of negotiable instruments. He received a favorable response. Subsequently, Chalmers prepared a bill based on his book, and Parliament passed it as the Bills of Exchange Act of 1882. In America, the National Conference of Commissioners on Uniform State Laws proposed a Negotiable Instruments Law in 1896, based in large measure on the prior English Bills of Exchange Act of 1882, but reflecting American commercial practice as it differed from the English. This act was the earliest complete success of the

National Conference, and all states adopted it by 1924.

The basic dilemma between justice and certainty was not resolved by this enactment. During the course of the twentieth century two developments took place: (1) the continued change in mercantile practice, and (2) divergent interpretations of particular points by various states. By the 1940's, therefore, it was apparent that the law was out of step with the times and that the divergent interpretations had to be brought together. In addition, it was felt that separate statutes on various areas of commercial law might profitably be combined in one large statute.

The American Law Institute and the National Conference of Commissioners on Uniform State Laws started, in 1945, to create a Uniform Commercial Code covering eight previously separate areas of commercial law, including negotiable paper. Its first official draft was published in 1952 and covered the subject matter of the Negotiable Instruments Law (1896), the Uniform Warehouse Receipts Act (1906), the Uniform Sales Act (1906), the Uniform Bills of Lading Act (1909), the Uniform Stock Transfer Act (1909), the Uniform Conditional Sales Act (1918), and the Uniform Trust Receipts Act (1933).

Subsequent drafts appeared based on changes suggested by myriad critics, and is now law in all states and most of it is law in Louisiana.

There is no reason to believe, of course, that this code will solve the basic conflict between justice and certainty. Surely commercial practices will change, and just as surely the law must change in order to reflect market conditions and facilitate commercial activity. To some extent the code incorporates a built-in factor to allow for change by stating, in various places, that the courts shall consider commercial standards in coming to decisions. Such terms as "good faith," "reasonableness," "honesty in fact," "observance of reasonable commercial standards," and "commercial reasonableness" are used to set standards in particular areas. These standards are, generally, the objective standards of the market place and not the subjective standards of a person's individual and private intention. One incisive comment on the code maintains that, in using such terms, it recognizes "as the legal norm for determining controversies the variant rules of conduct observed in actual transaction of business." To some extent, then, commercial change can be automatically incorporated into the law as commercial practices change the nature or content of particular commercial standards.

This, therefore, is the eternal task of commercial law: to determine the approaches and rules that govern commercial transactions; to reflect commercial practice, where its effect is beneficial or at least benign, in order to achieve the goal of a legal climate in which commerce can flourish; but not to ignore its duty to strike down practices that are inimical to the public interest.

CHAPTER XIII

BUSINESS ORGANIZATIONS

The modern business corporation is the legal response to the economic need for a means to amass the tremendous capital needed in modern business. It is a composite of three elements—the concepts of the corporate entity, joint stock, and limited liability—each of which stems from a different source.

The concept of entity is that the corporation is a legal person. It may sue and be sued in its own name, own and transfer property, enter into contracts, commit torts and crimes, and do all other things that its nonmaterial nature permits. Because the corporation is an entity, it may be established to exist perpetually.

Joint stock enables shareholders to transfer their shares during their lives or at death. It is this concept that makes the ownership of a corporation divisible into small shares and, therefore, enables it to draw its capital from a multitude of relatively small investors.

Limited liability protects shareholders against personal ruin if the corporation fails financially. The shareholders will lose no more than their initial investment commitment or, at most, some excess, fixed by statute, over that investment.

Only the second of these features, joint stock, is essential to the accumulation of large amounts of capital. The theory of entity, although not essential, is desirable, for to require the joinder of all shareholders in suits, contracts, and other business of a corporation would be unwieldy if not impossible. Even this, however, might have been accomplished under a theory of representation related to that of a trust or an agency. Limited liability, likewise, is not an absolute necessity. If shareholders were merely held immune from personal liability until corporate assets were exhausted, they would have a high degree of immunity from liability in actual practice if not in theory.

EARLY ENTITY CONCEPTS

A corporation is a distinct legal personality. As an entity, a corporation has three basic attributes: it can buy, hold, and dispose of property in its own name; it can contract in its own name; and it can sue and be sued in its own name. A corporation needs neither limited liability nor joint stock. These are attributes of business corporations; but most charitable and all municipal or governmental corporations do very well without them, because such corporations have no shareholders.

The Roman Concept

A legal entity, created by express action of the state, was known to Roman law as a *universitas*. Cities, colonies, brotherhoods of priests, and groups of artisans achieved that status. Some elementary forms of business associations also were given corporate status in certain cases, particularly in ventures such as salt mining, ore extraction, and tax collection.

Churches and Universities

Another source of the concept of entity was the medieval Church. Pollock and Maitland consider the theological notion of the Church as the mystical body of Christ an important factor in the development of the corporate idea.

The common law early recognized that property given to the Church no longer belonged to the patron who donated it. Where control lay within the Church, however, was a problem. Earliest theory avowed that the property belonged to God or to the patron saint of the parish. The clergyman in charge, therefore, was the rector, or administrator, of the property who did not own the property in his own right, but was accountable to the Church in the person of his successor in office. If, for instance, an abbott or bishop made an improper alienation of land under his control, it could be regained not by the monks (who were legally dead), but by his successor.

But where did the ownership lie in the interval of time between the death of one official and the installation of his successor? For a while, title was said to be held "by the walls of the church" or by the "body or the bride of the Redeemer," but this gave way to the view that the Church itself owned the property as part of the *ecclesia universalis* (church universal, indicating the church as a person). The idea of the *ecclesia universalis* is also related to the status of the early English universities, Oxford and Cambridge, which were treated as entities because of ancient usage. The relationship was not in function but in the Roman concept of the *universitas* as an entity which, being nonmaterial and fictitious, was not subject to corporal punishment in this world or the next.

From all this ecclesiastical theory, the common law had to devise a concept for dealing with the mundane interests of the Church. The courts apparently seized upon the idea of representation: the clergy were in a relationship to their property, their Church, and their flocks which made them a type of father or agent or guardian. In that position the Church was, like a minor, sheltered by the courts and given their protection. The idea was not purely corporate, but it had some elements of corporateness.

Boroughs and Towns

Before the fourteenth century, boroughs were corporations by prescription, or ancient usage; and after that time, by charter from the Crown. Boroughs had a number of corporate characteristics, including the power to hold borough courts, to compel members of the borough to buy and sell there and to tax their trade, to govern themselves (within limits), to form merchant guilds, and to own land and perhaps some chattels.

Guilds

There were two types of guilds dealing in business: merchant and craft. Merchant guilds were monopolies of retail trade; craft guilds were associations of craftsmen with power to regulate their memberships.

Merchant Guilds. When a borough merchants' trade became sufficient to justify his membership, he joined a guild. It was an organization separate from the borough or town government, but its influential members might hold offices in both groups. The guild's by-laws reached beyond its membership, regulating trade within the boroughs, and it could buy commodities outside the borough for local sale and profit.

Merchant guilds were powerful from the thirteenth to the fifteenth century. After this period their power decreased, because trade ceased to be a monopoly of the towns. Their contribution to corporate theory was their regulation of borough commerce and transaction of business for a common profit.

Craft Guilds. The second quarter of the twelfth century marked the appearance of the craft guilds. During the reign of Henry II they were sometimes given charters which made them separate, administratively, from their towns. When Richard I (1189–1199) succeeded Henry, however, craft guilds were once more subordinated to town management.

The purpose of the craft guilds, as distinguished from that of the merchant guilds, was economic, not governmental. Their object was to create a class of workmen competent to serve the public. They supervised apprenticeships in their respective crafts, regulated standards of work, and exercised effective control over their own members.

With the loss of power by the merchant guilds after the fifteenth century and the breakdown of borough control over borough commerce, craft guilds expanded. Masters in crafts became managers of businesses. They left their workbenches and became, in effect, members of a monopoly in their crafts. The economic distinction between working artisans and capital-owning masters was recognized by the "livery company," a term derived from the distinctive dress which only the masters were entitled to wear. Masters, who ran their separate businesses, also controlled trade in their crafts by means of regulations binding on all members of these companies.

Many livery companies were granted incorporation or the equivalent by the king. The practice of incorporating these companies dates back at least to 1407 when Henry IV granted the privilege to the haberdashers. The movement gained momentum with the incorporation of the fishmongers in 1433, the vintners in 1437, the merchant tailors in 1466, and the carpenters in 1477. In the sixteenth century, companies of foreign merchants were incorporated. In each of these companies members traded on their separate accounts, but the group had corporate powers. The organization presaged the modern corporation in that its formation was voluntary, it had a common seal, and it could sue and be sued as a unit.

Commenda and Societas

On the Continent, other forms of business organization were also used. The *commenda* resembled a modern limited partnership. It combined capital and management by providing for investment of money in return for a share of the profits. The investors did not manage the business, and they had limited liability; the active partners controlled the business. It was not, however, an entity.

The *societas* had some features of corporateness, such as the ability to enter into a contract in its own name. However, liability of the members was unlimited; each could act for the group, and they were not complete juristic persons.

JOINT STOCK COMPANIES

By the sixteenth century, English overseas trade had sufficiently developed to require large capital structures. The joint stock company was devised to meet this need. The first of these were, properly speaking, regulated companies. They received charters from the Crown for their overseas activities, but the members traded for their own profit, and the company itself did not trade. They resembled the guilds in many ways, including their regulatory powers over members. In addition, they were given governmental powers in overseas areas in which they traded. One of the earliest English companies was the Russia Company, formed in 1555. More permanent was the East India Company, formed in 1600. In its earlier form, separate investments were made for each voyage, but in 1613, stock began to be subscribed for a period of years; and in 1657 permanent joint stock was offered. With these changes, the right to trade on the members' private accounts disappeared. When transferability of shares was added to corporate trading, the joint stock company of eighteenth century England was complete.

About the same time, chartered monopolies in trade were extended to companies in England itself. The Mines Royal obtained its charter in 1568; so did the Mineral and Battery Works. During the seventeenth century, charters were granted to the Governor and Company of Copper Mines in England, the Fishery Company, the Company of White Papermakers in England, the Royal Lutestring Company, and others. These companies, distinguished from those trading overseas, had no governmental powers. Their monopolies, moreover, were protected only against competition by other corporations. Individuals could compete with them.

Joint stock companies were of various types. Those dealing overseas uniformly acted under royal charters. Domestic joint stock companies often were voluntary associations formed by contract without charters. The charter was needed in order to achieve perpetuity and, presumably, limited liability. Some charters, nevertheless, did not grant perpetual existence, and limited liability (as will be explained) did not mean what it does today. Without incorporation, vexing problems could arise in suing or being sued, for companies would be treated as if they were partnerships in which all members must be joined. Some of the early American colonies were formed as chartered joint stock companies.

LIMITED LIABILITY

Today, limited liability means that shareholders are not responsible for the debts of the corporation beyond the amount of their subscriptions. Often this is considered a consequence of the theory of entity. That theory, however, supports only the proposition that the debts of the corporation are separate from the debts of its shareholders. The separateness of corporate obligations was observed as early as 1441 in England, and in a 1680 case it was observed that to hold otherwise would not be consistent with the essential nature of a corporate body.

However, in those days members were assessable, and the corporation could be ordered to require its members to make good its debts under penalty of contempt. This was the procedure called leviation, the subject of a 1671 case.

Until the eighteenth century corporations were not created for business purposes. The closest approximation to the business corporation was the chartered joint stock company, to which limited liability was sometimes granted. The owners of a nonchartered joint stock company were subject to unlimited liability, in the manner of a partnership.

Out of a general movement against joint stock companies, however, a new device arose. The event which brought this about was the infamous South Sea Bubble. The South Sea Company, a chartered joint stock company, took government securities in exchange for its stock in order to assume most of the national debt. Owing to a generally speculative market and to speculation in South Sea Company stock, the price of the stock rose tremendously, and as a result, the Company had to offer less and less of its stock for government securities of a given value. Other companies, despite their differing legal purposes and whether or not they were chartered, saw an opportunity for profit in this market and offered their stock for government securities. In consequence, the price of South Sea stock was depressed. The South Sea Company then obtained the passage of the Bubble Act of 1720, forbidding companies to act without a charter or, if chartered, outside their chartered purposes. The act was meant to protect the South

Sea Company's monopoly; its effect, however, was a severe market crash caused by judicial investigations into the activities of competitors. Stocks of all joint stock companies fell in the general decline of stock prices.

The Bubble Act cast a pall over promotions in the form of joint stock companies, and other modes of organization were sought. One approach was to form a partnership but to attempt to permit the assignment of a partner's interest. Another and more successful device was to draw a deed of trust appointing certain individuals trustees (managers) of the fund for the purposes set forth in the instrument. In some cases, provisions were inserted, making the interests of the investors transferable. In addition, some trusts provided that investors were not liable to third parties for the debts of the trusts. This provision was effective, in equity, when third persons, aware of the disclaimer of liability, extended credit to the trust and tried to collect from its investors. This disclaimer is the source of the English use of the word "limited" after a company's name.

Organizations formed for public benefit rather than for private profit were construed to lie outside the intendment of the Bubble Act. During the succeeding century, therefore, to avoid technical infringement of the Bubble Act, some phrase or clause would be inserted to imply a public or beneficial purpose.

The Bubble Act was finally repealed in 1825. The repealing act, however, provided for incorporation with unlimited liability only. The pressure for limited liability and for the ability to act as a joint stock company without a charter continued until 1834, when the Trading Companies Act legally recognized the demand and enabled joint stock companies to sue through their officers. This act and parts of the 1825 act were repealed in 1837, and new provisions were adopted, giving limited liability in amounts varying with each company and not fixed by the amount invested. Still, however, the administering Board of Trade granted privileges only to organizations that could demonstrate some public advantage from their operations.

The Companies Act of 1862 (which followed a series of intermediate acts) was the final culmination of this legislative development. It provided for a formal method of incorporation as a joint stock company with or without limited liability. If there were more than twenty members, they had to become a corporation; but if there were fewer than seven members, they had to be a partnership.

AMERICAN CORPORATIONS

American business corporation law does not owe much to English law. Indeed, our law on this subject was developed at an earlier date and was cited as an example by the English to their Parliament; it was a causative factor in modern English law.

After the American Revolution, it was generally understood that limited liability was an attribute of the formally incorporated business organization and that unlimited liability was one of the risks of the joint stock enterprise. Before 1800, about 330 charters of incorporation were granted in America. They were concentrated in New England, and were usually in public-interest ventures such as turnpikes, water companies, and insurance, rather than completely private-profit enterprises. During that time, little bias had grown up against the corporate form of doing business, apparently because dissolution had not been accompanied by injury to creditors.

The doctrine of limited liability (unless the statute creating the corporation provided otherwise) was clearly established in the leading case of *Spear v. Grant,* in 1819. Considerable legislative doubt, however, existed with respect to the propriety of limited liability when applied to purely private-profit institutions. Massachusetts, for instance, adopted and maintained a policy of unlimited liability for such ventures from 1809 to 1830. First the creditor had to exhaust corporate property; and if that did not satisfy his claim, he could levy on the property of individual shareholders. In the case of banks, this era saw the beginning of shareholders' liability for double the amount of their subscriptions, a policy that continued until the 1930's.

Other states had varied legislative policies on the subject of limited liability. After 1816 Connecticut and New Hampshire granted limited liability in all cases and Maine did so after 1823. Rhode Island did not abandon unlimited liability until 1847. New York was partial to a policy of double liability, but Pennsylvania, except for one year, was an advocate of limited liability. However, because early Pennsylvania legislatures granted corporate charters only for nonindustrial purposes, the question was relatively unimportant.

In general, the adoption of a policy of limited liability awaited some protection of corporate creditors. The courts developed means of preventing premature distribution of corporate assets among the shareholders. The legislatures prohibited the invasion of capital by setting up restrictions on the declaration of dividends. Liability was imposed on shareholders who failed to pay in full for their shares of stock. Experiments with extensive publicity requirements were conducted, in the hope that creditors might be advised of the financial strengths and weaknesses of corporations with which they proposed to deal. These and other financial safeguards were devised in the second quarter of the nineteenth century, in order that the dual aims of creditor protection and limited liability could be met. The price of limited liability was respect for the capital stock account.

The classical mode of incorporation was, in this country, by special legislative act for each incorporation. The movement toward general acts started in 1811 in New York. By complying with automatic statutory provisions instead of making separate petitions to the legislature, corporations could be formed in certain businesses if limited to $100,000 in capital and to a corporate life of twenty or fewer years. By 1870 all states had general incorporation acts, but restrictions on corporate purposes and on maximum capitalization were not removed until the beginning of the twentieth century. Until that time, corporate charters were granted only in areas of activity that the legislatures desired to foster.

Modern business corporation law is uniformly based on detailed state statutes. After the Civil War and until the 1930's, many jurisdictions attempted to induce promoters to incorporate in their own states. The advantages offered—including lower taxes and fewer restrictions on management discretion—led to increasing diversity in the corporation laws of the states. In the 1930's, a movement toward uniformity based on sound legal principles began with the Illinois Business Corporation Act of 1933, followed by the Pennsylvania Act of the same year. In 1946, the Committee on Corporate Laws of the American Bar Association published a proposed Model Business Corporation Act which was adopted by thirty-five states and influenced the law in many other states. The current Revised Business Corporation Act was published in 1985.

Corporation law still, however, differs to some extent among the several states. As with all uniform acts, the fact that the same or similar legislation is adopted by the states does not mean that their courts will interpret the legislation in the same way. Therefore, in addition to the statute, the case interpretation of the statute must be examined in each state or, if there are no cases on the point, case law of the leading states in corporate law, such as Delaware and New York, must be studied.

CORPORATE STATUS AS A PRIVILEGE

In essence the state determines whether or not a particular group shall be treated as an entity, or corporation. Grant of that status, however, has historically had its price. The price has been some return benefit to the state. The nature of the benefit has varied with the values of the state involved. Rome, as was noted, granted corporate status to groups involved in salt mining, gold and silver mining, and collection of taxes. Salt, a scarce commodity until very recent times, is essential to human life. Gold and silver, it was thought, added to the wealth of the nation. This theory, which spelled the undoing of Spain which sought to increase its wealth by taking precious metals from the New World, was realized to be wrong only with the growth of the modern science of economics.

England, denied these commodities, increased its wealth in a true sense by spurring trade, commerce, and manufactures. Tax collection, then as now, is essential to the nation.

English corporations also benefitted the state. Livery companies were essential in spurring manufactures, and chartered joint stock companies fostered foreign trade. The English mistake occurred, however, in adhering to the idea that corporateness involved monopoly when they started to incorporate individual companies in the sixteenth century. It was this feature of corporations that caused Adam Smith, in his *Wealth of Nations* (1776), to inveigh against them except where large masses of capital were needed or risk had to be spread.

Until the late nineteenth century, American incorporations were guarded by the legislatures. Only certain purposes were permitted, and those were the ones the legislatures desired to foster. The size of corporations was limited by restrictions on capital. The first American corporations for business purposes were in New England. The reason is not far to seek. While the Middle Atlantic and Southern states found high profits in agriculture, these were less obtainable from the rocky soil of New England. Trade was its way of life. Textiles, the first application of the factory system, required large sums of capital, and as a means to increase the wealth of the New England states was a legislative favorite. Until the early nineteenth century corporations were formed only where there was a public need and the state was too poor to supply the service—turnpikes, waterworks, and banks.

Toward the end of the nineteenth century, however, business came to be considered a good thing in itself. Business created wealth, jobs, goods and services, and these were by definition desirable. The United States was expanding to fill its western plains. Its manufacturers were making it an exporter of goods rather than an importer. The legislative response was to remove the lid and permit unlimited capitalizations for "any legal purpose." Today the law remains the same, but there is much troubled thinking over the nature of the obligation that business corporations owe to the public.

PARTNERSHIPS

The partnership is one of the oldest forms of doing business. It is found in ancient Babylonian and Jewish law, in Roman law, and throughout the Middle Ages. Nevertheless, it still creates a great number of conceptual and practical difficulties.

A startling number of questions can arise from the simple statement that a partnership is an association of persons in business for profit. Can a partnership sue or be sued in its own name? Who owns partnership property, the partners or the partnership? Can partnership creditors sue the partners directly for the debts of the partnership? Can partners sell their interests in partnership property? Can partners use partnership property for their individual purposes? Can the act of one partner bind the partnership to liability in contract or to liability in tort? Is an incoming or outgoing partner liable for earlier partnership debts?

Entity and Aggregate Theories

The basic and underlying question for a legal system to answer is whether it wishes the partnership to be treated as an entity or as an aggregation of individuals. If it is an entity, it can sue and be sued in its own name, own the partnership property, probably be solely liable for its debts (although leviation may apply here), and have sole control of its property. Its partners then are agents of the partnership and can bind it to tort or contract liability in accordance with agency principles.

If a partnership is an aggregation of individuals, it cannot sue or be sued in its own name (all the partners must be joined in suit), the partners own partnership property and can sell their interests in it, and they are liable for partnership debts directly.

Neither approach is fully satisfactory. No one would contend that the limited liability of an entity should be an attribute of a partnership that is not formed as a limited partnership, and leviation is too cumbersome a mode of collection by creditors. However, if a single partner could sell his interest in specific partnership property, as he could under the aggregate theory, he could deprive the partnership of the use of its most essential asset and so frustrate the other partners.

Partnership law was in a state of confusion until the beginning of the twentieth century. As early as 1693, for instance, it was decided that partners owned partnership property as joint tenants. It followed that since each partner owned an undivided interest in each parcel of partnership property, whether real or personal, the creditor of an individual partner could levy on his debtor's interest in partnership property. Although the common-law joint tenant could voluntarily sell his interest in jointly owned property, it was later established that a partner could not voluntarily sell his interest in partnership property. The common-law joint tenancy, in other words, was inadequate to handle the problems created by the partnership. Other problems of equal difficulty included the relative rights of individual and partnership creditors in individual and partnership assets when the partnership was liquidated, whether the executor of a deceased partner had a right to join in winding up a partnership, the rights of partners among themselves during the operation of the business, and the liabilities of incoming partners.

The Uniform Partnership Act

The National Conference of Commissioners on Uniform State Laws began to consider a Uniform Partnership Act in 1902. The first draft was to be based on the entity rather than on the aggregate theory. The entity theory was not only the apparent approach of the law merchant, but it was, hopefully, a solution to the vexing problem of a partner's rights in specific partnership property: by ownership and control of partnership property in the partnership itself, as an entity, creditors of individual partners could not attach it.

Dean William Draper Lewis, of the University of Pennsylvania Law School, assumed responsibility for drafting the act in 1910. He believed that the entity theory would create as many problems as it solved, particularly in the area of liability of partners. The problem was how, under the entity theory, partners were to be made liable for partnership debts. There were three alternatives: first, to treat them as co-principals on all partnership contracts; second, to treat them as sureties; third, to make them parties to an implied contract to supply the partnership with sufficient money to satisfy the third party.

Each of these courses of action was unsatisfactory. The co-principal theory was a complete fiction. The surety theory would not provide for partners' liability for partnership torts (for which everyone admitted they were and should be liable), and the implied contract theory would mean a return to the leviation procedure, which had been repudiated in corporation law for almost a century.

These and other questions were answered by taking an intermediate approach. When necessary, the proposed act treated the partnership as an entity or as an aggregation of individuals. The aggregate theory was dominant, however.

Under the Act, the partnership can be sued in its own name, which is an application of entity theory. It is provided, however, that unless individual partners are also sued and served with process, only partnership assets can be touched. A like theory was adopted for partnership property, for ownership of the property was placed in the partnership. Therefore, no partner can sell or encumber it, and it is not subject to the claims of the creditors of individual partners. The interest of the partners is solely in the partnership business, not in its assets. In order to give a creditor of an individual partner some recourse against the debtor partner's interest in the partnership, the creditor can obtain a court order turning over his debtor's share of partnership profits to him until he is paid off or until the partnership comes to its natural termination, at which time he can attach the debtor's interest in partnership property directly.

The aggregate theory was recognized by providing that partners may be sued directly for partnership contract debts and that they are directly liable for partnership torts, reserving to the partners a right of contribution from their co-partners for payments in excess of their proportionate shares.

The Uniform Partnership Act has profoundly influenced the course of the law. The act illustrates the difficulty of relying on the direct application of common-law doctrines to solve business problems. On the other hand, it demonstrates the fact that judicious building on the foundation of the common law, rejecting that which is obsolete or inapplicable, changing that which is malleable, and developing new principles where required can foster sound legal growth and consolidation.

Limited Partnerships

A limited partnership has two types of partners, limited and general. The limited partners contribute capital and are not responsible for partnership debts or torts. The most they can lose is their investment. The general partners manage the business and are personally liable for partnership debts and torts. The limited partners are not permitted to engage in management. If they do, they become general partners and are unlimitedly liable.

The limited partnership was unknown to the common law of England and the United States. It originated in medieval Europe in an arrangement known as the *commenda*. One group contributed capital that was managed by another. The capital contributors received the bulk of the profits but were not personally liable to creditors. A French ordinance of 1673 recognized the limited partnership (*la Société en commandité*) and it was introduced into Louisiana, a state that had inherited the French civil law.

New York, the first state to do so, authorized limited partnerships by statute in 1822. Fourteen states followed. Chancellor Kent, in the third volume of his 1826 *Commentaries on American Law,* observed that these statutes were " * * * supposed to be well calculated to bring dormant capital into active and useful employment * * *."

Limited partnerships filled a need. State legislators could control the purpose and size of corporations in their acts of incorporation. Partnerships could be voluntarily formed in any business, and their size was limited by the size of the fortunes of the partners. In the middle were persons who wanted to invest in the wide range of non-corporate business, but who did not want to participate in management and who feared the possibility of unlimited liability. The limited partnership provided a way to open up investments for this group, and to eliminate their fears of unlimited liability.

On the public policy side, limited partnerships did not create the spectre of massive size. Limited liability was permissible because there would be at least one unlimitedly liable general partner.

The first Uniform Limited Partnership Act was proposed in 1916, and the current Revised Uniform Limited Partnership Act was proposed in 1976. That Act is on its way to universal adoption by the states.

A number of states have special statutory provisions for "close corporations." Close corporations are those with a limited number of shareholders, usually fewer than thirty, and whose shares are not traded on the open market. They are often called "incorporated partnerships." They have certain advantages such as enabling investors more easily to pass their interests on to their heirs, and to achieve certain advantages under the tax code.

INDEX

EQUITY
Basis of jurisdiction, 17–18
Distinguished from common law, 17–19
Jury not used in, 52, 67–68
Merger with law, 19

FEUDALISM
See also Real Property
Basic early values, 10
Economic and political bases, 134
End of military purpose, 135
Frankalmoign tenure, 137–138
Knight's service, 135
Primogeniture, origin and effects, 141–142
Seisin,
    Concept, 142–143
    Effect on wills of land, 172
    Remainders and reversions, in, 151–153
Socage tenure, 138
Subinfeudation,
        Generally, 26, 145
        Curtailed, 147–149
        Opposition to, reasons for, 145–147
Substitution, 144–145
Tenants in sergeanty, 137
Tenants in service and demesne, 26
Villeinage,
    Freeman's estate in, 140
    Villeinage, as a status, 138–140

GREAT COUNCIL
Composition, 9, 28
Functions, 28
Household, 28
Origin, 9

JUDGES
Church courts, in, 71, 89
Commissioners of Oyer and Terminer, 29
Earliest true, 89

†